This Book Belongs to

\-\-\-\-\-\-\-\-\-\-\-\-\-\-\-\-\-\-\-\-\-\-\-\-\-\-\-\-\-\-\-\-\-\-\-\-\-\-\-\-\-\-\-\-\-\-\-\-\-\-\-\-

© 2018 All rights Reserved

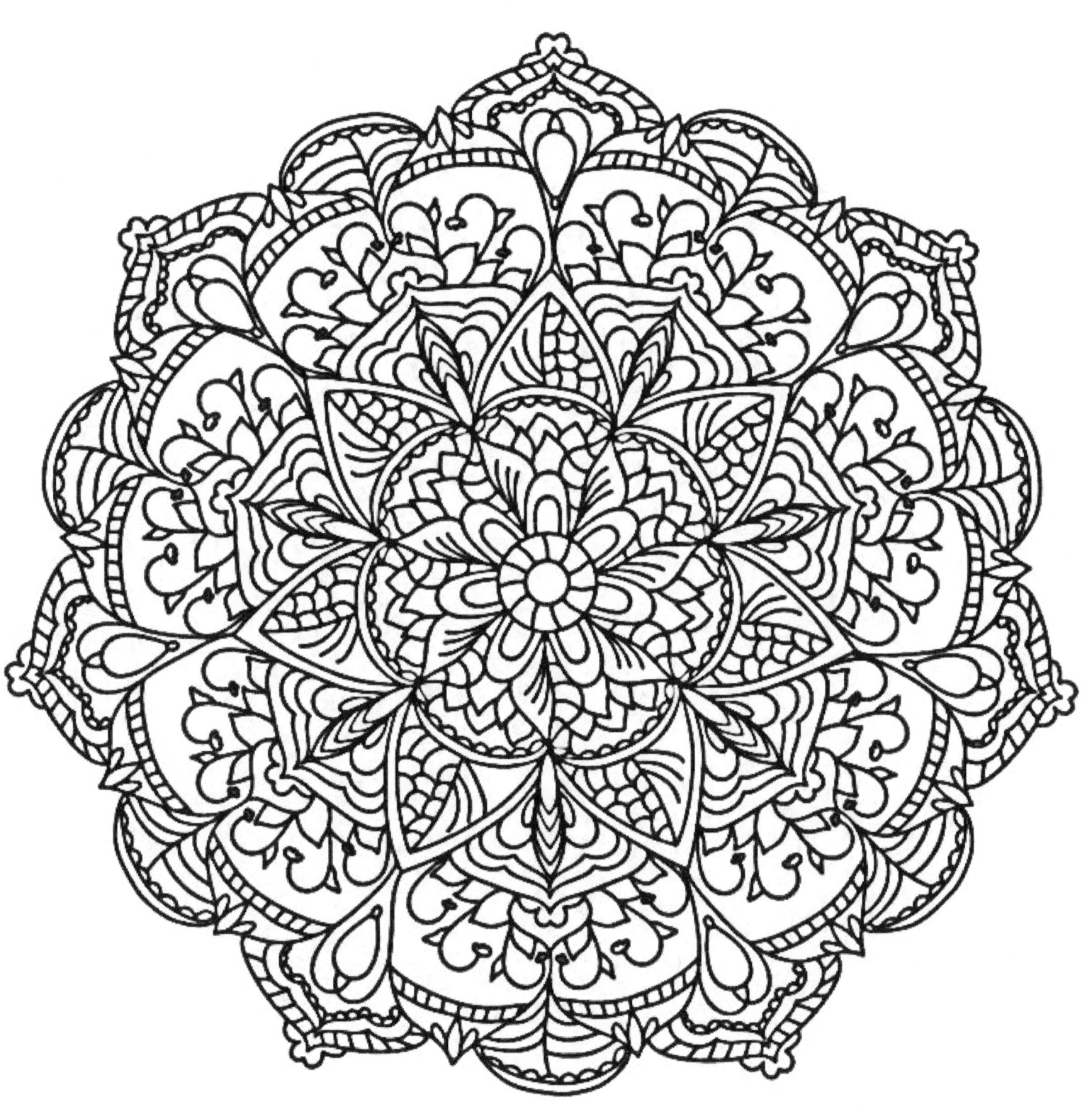

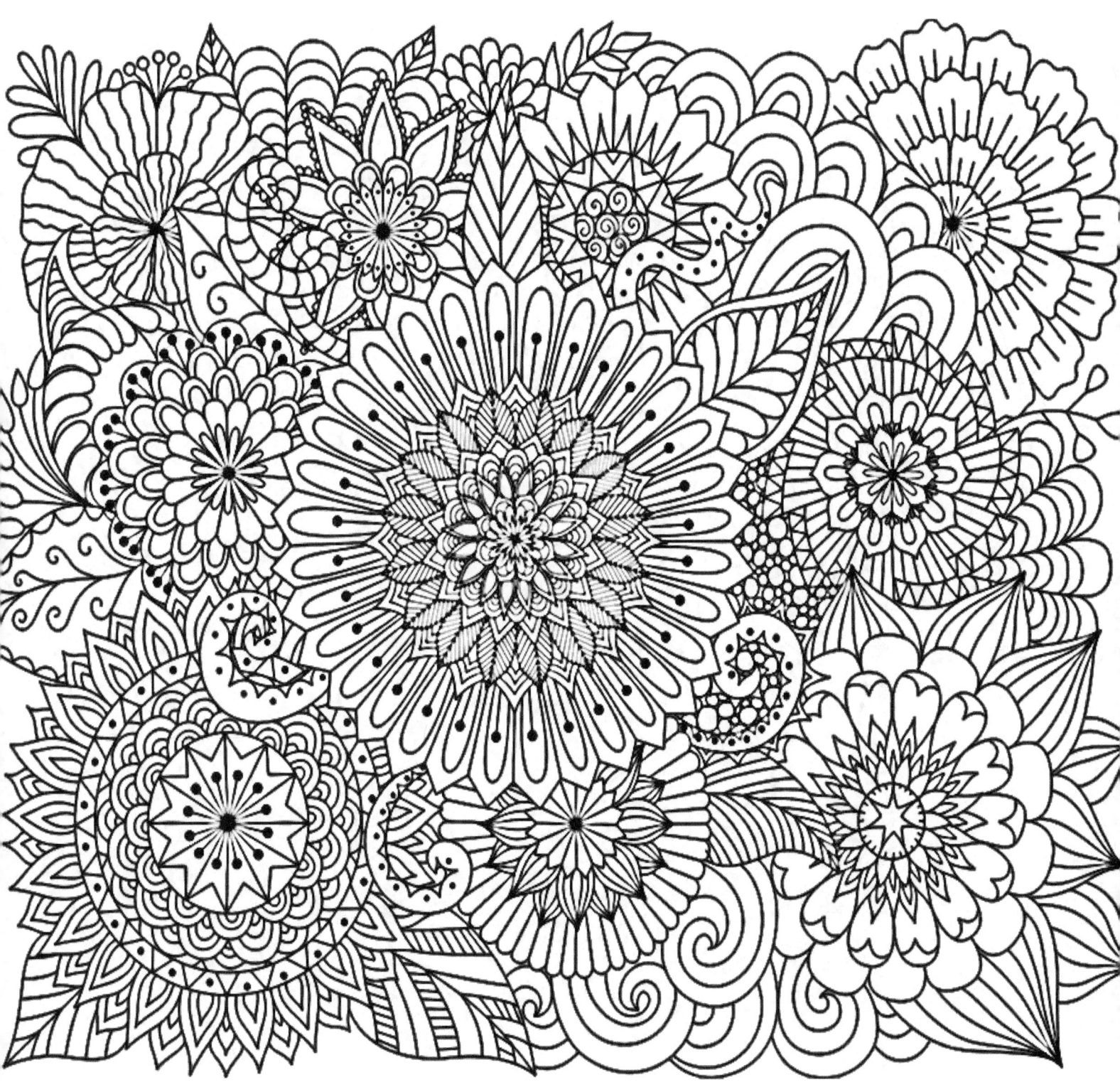

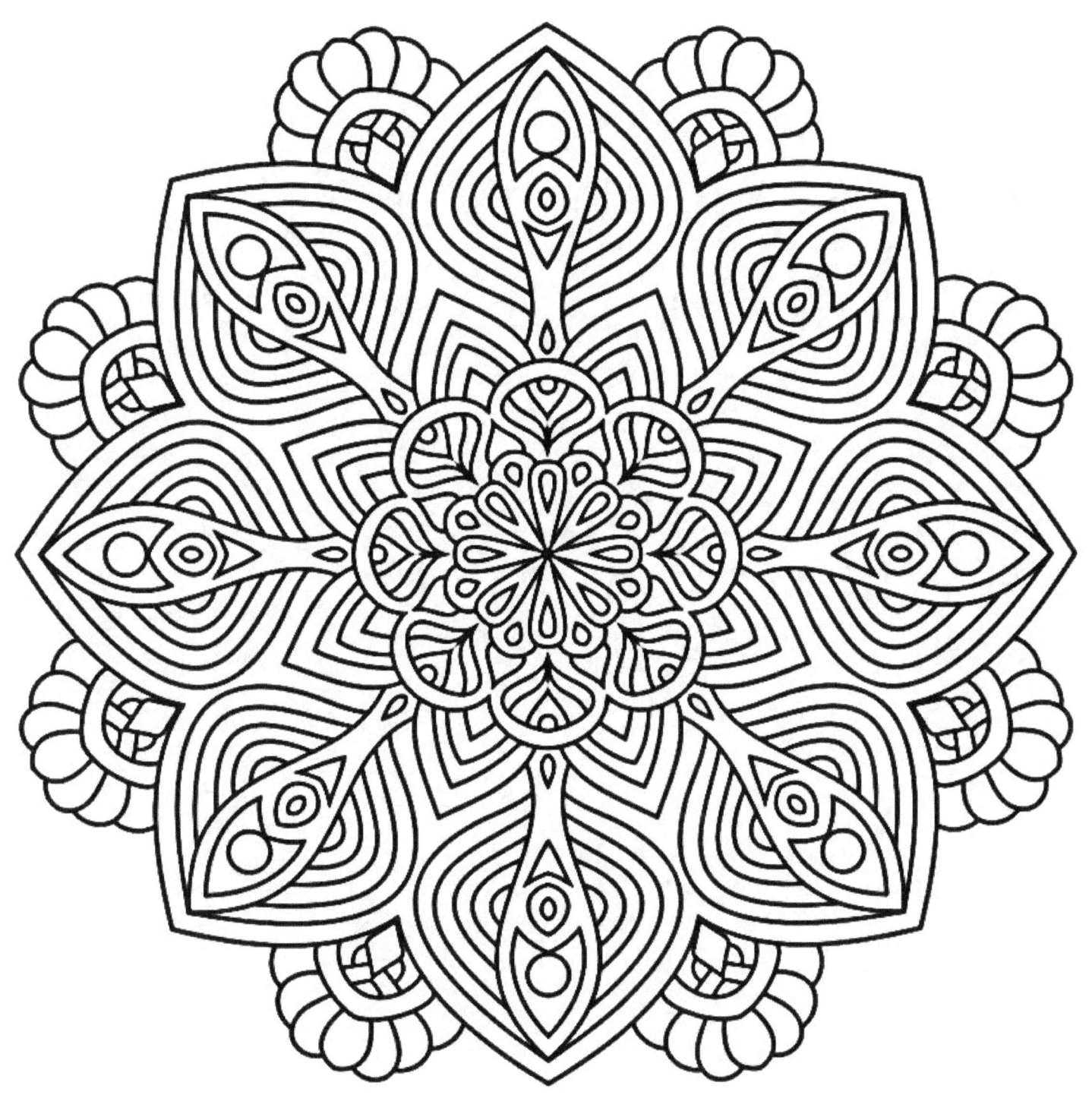

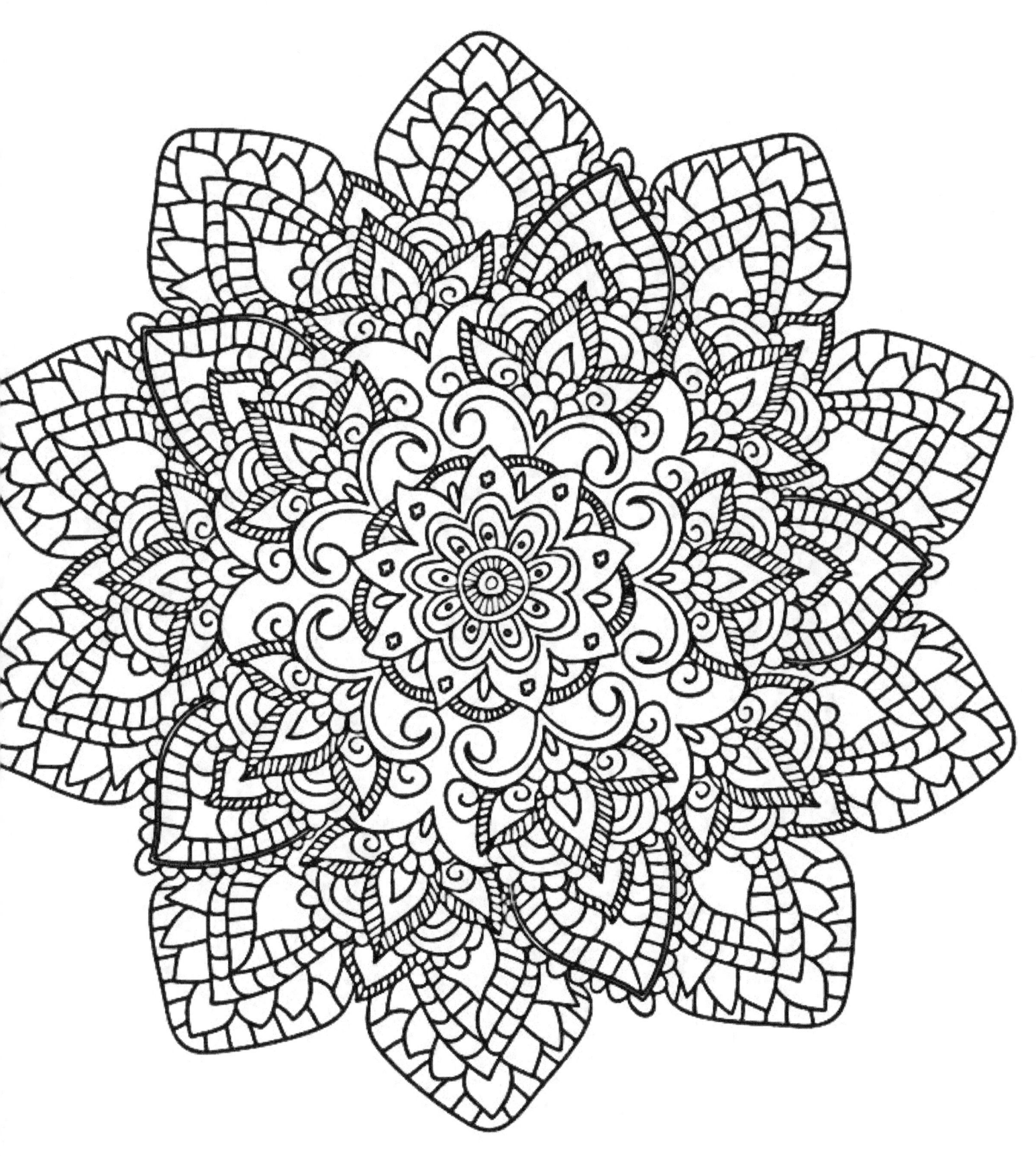

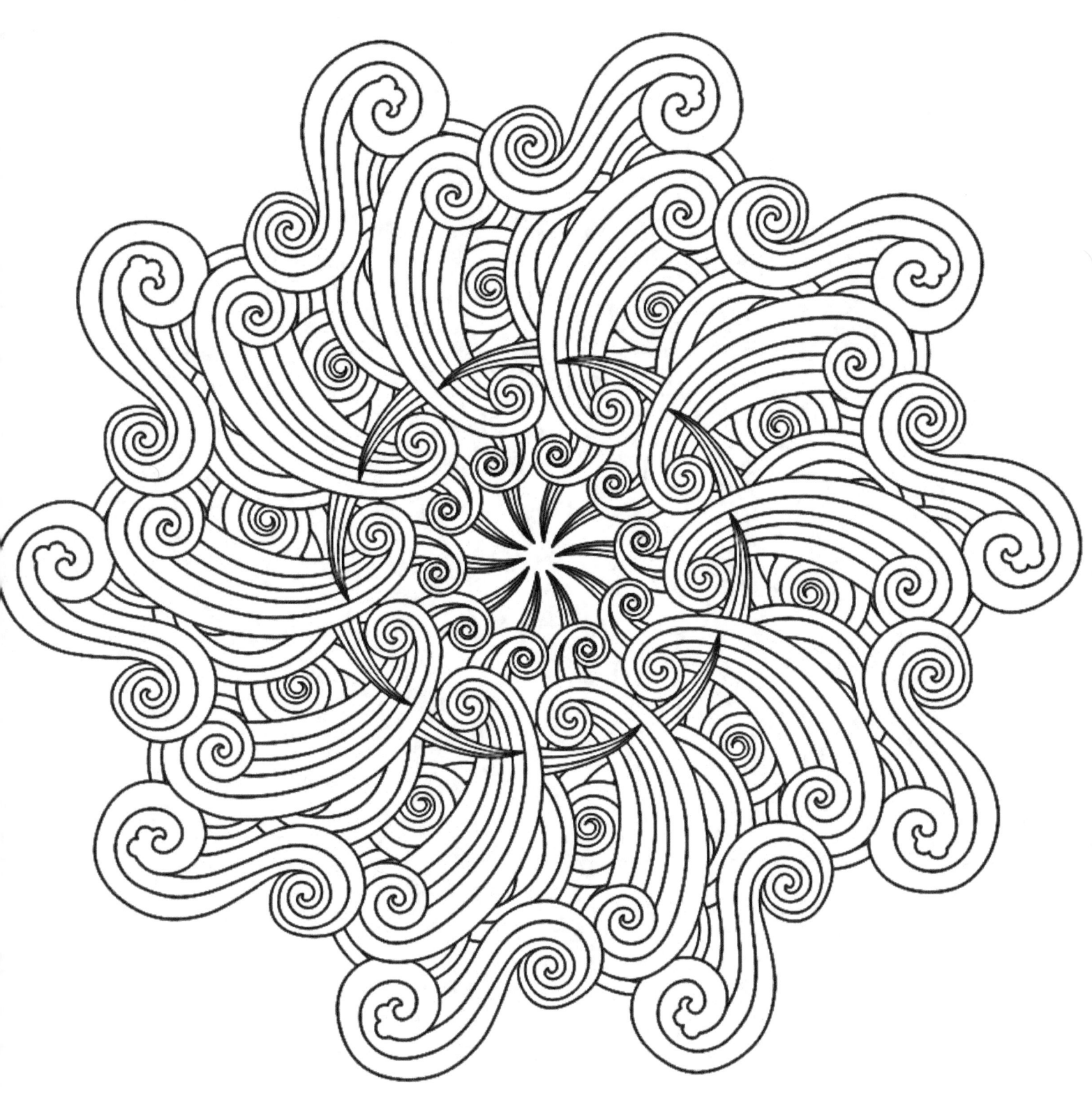

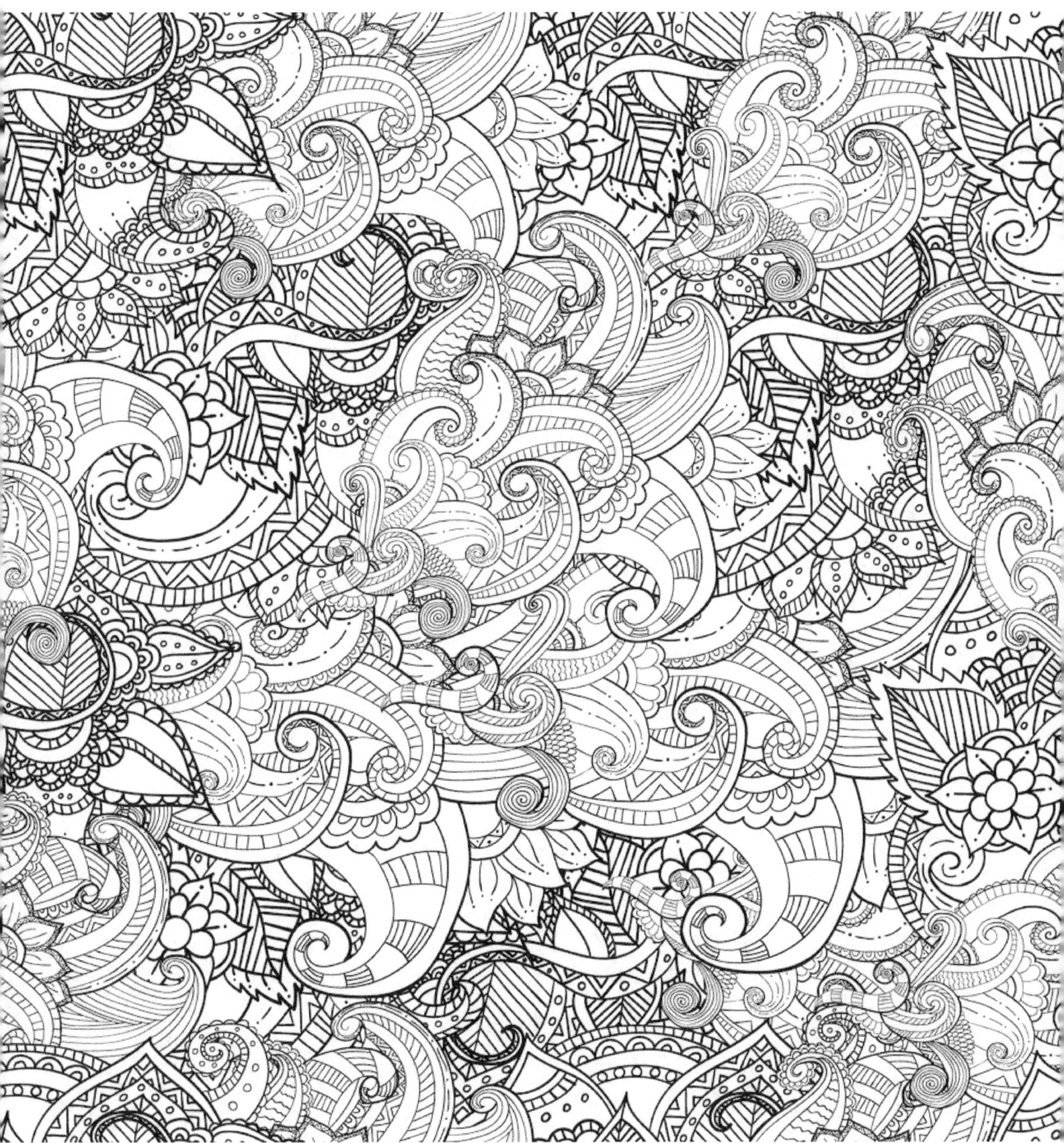

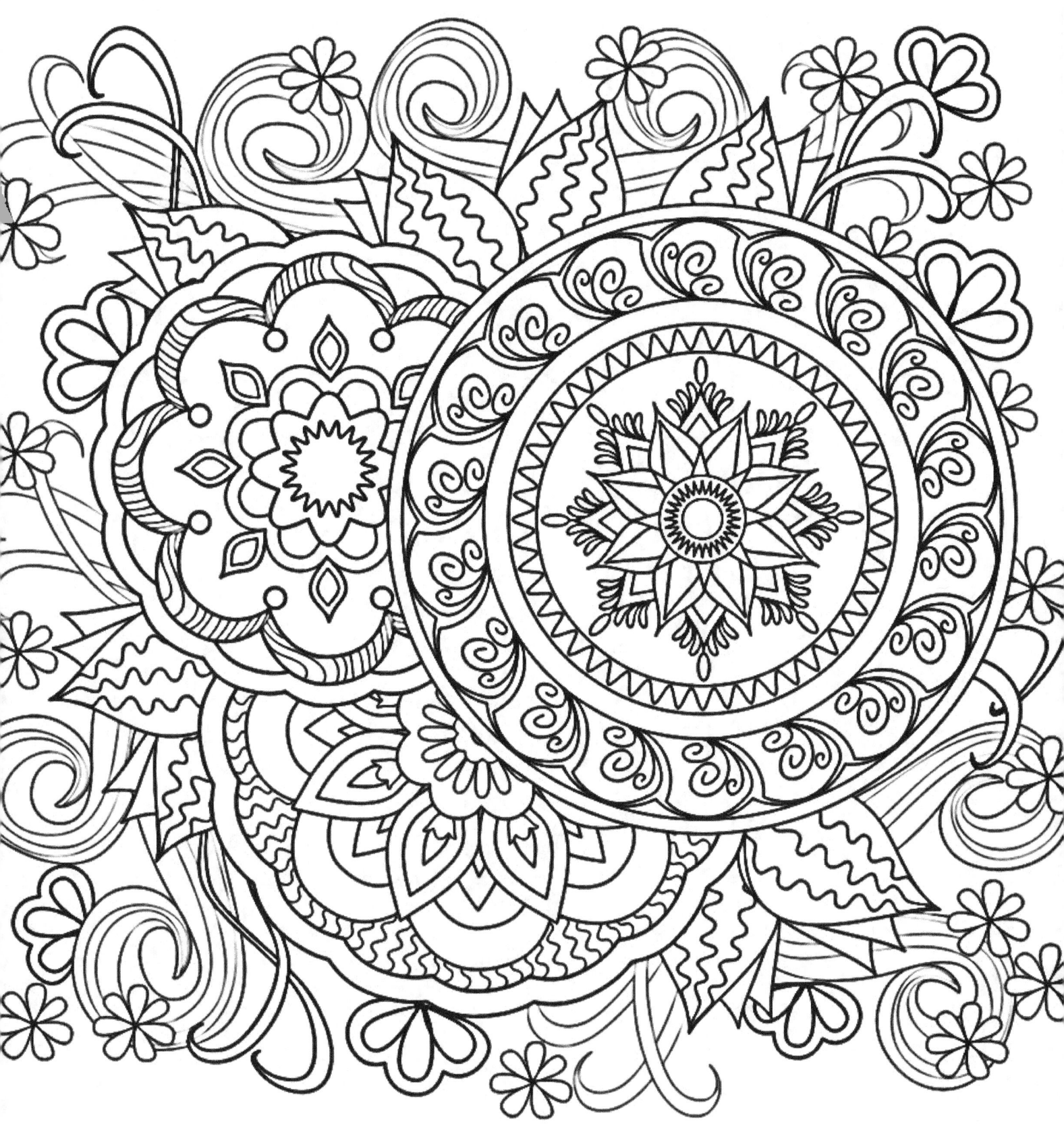

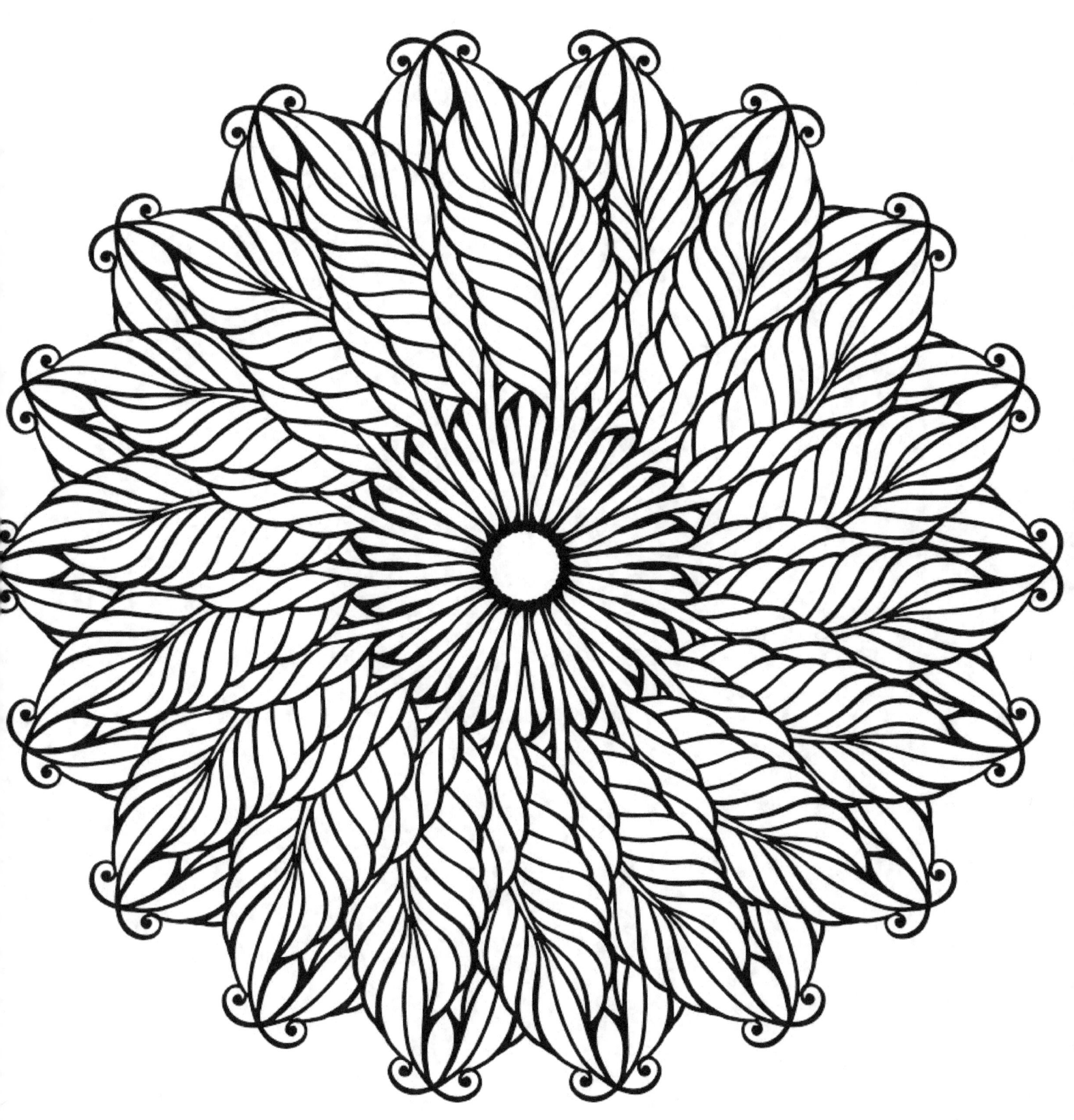

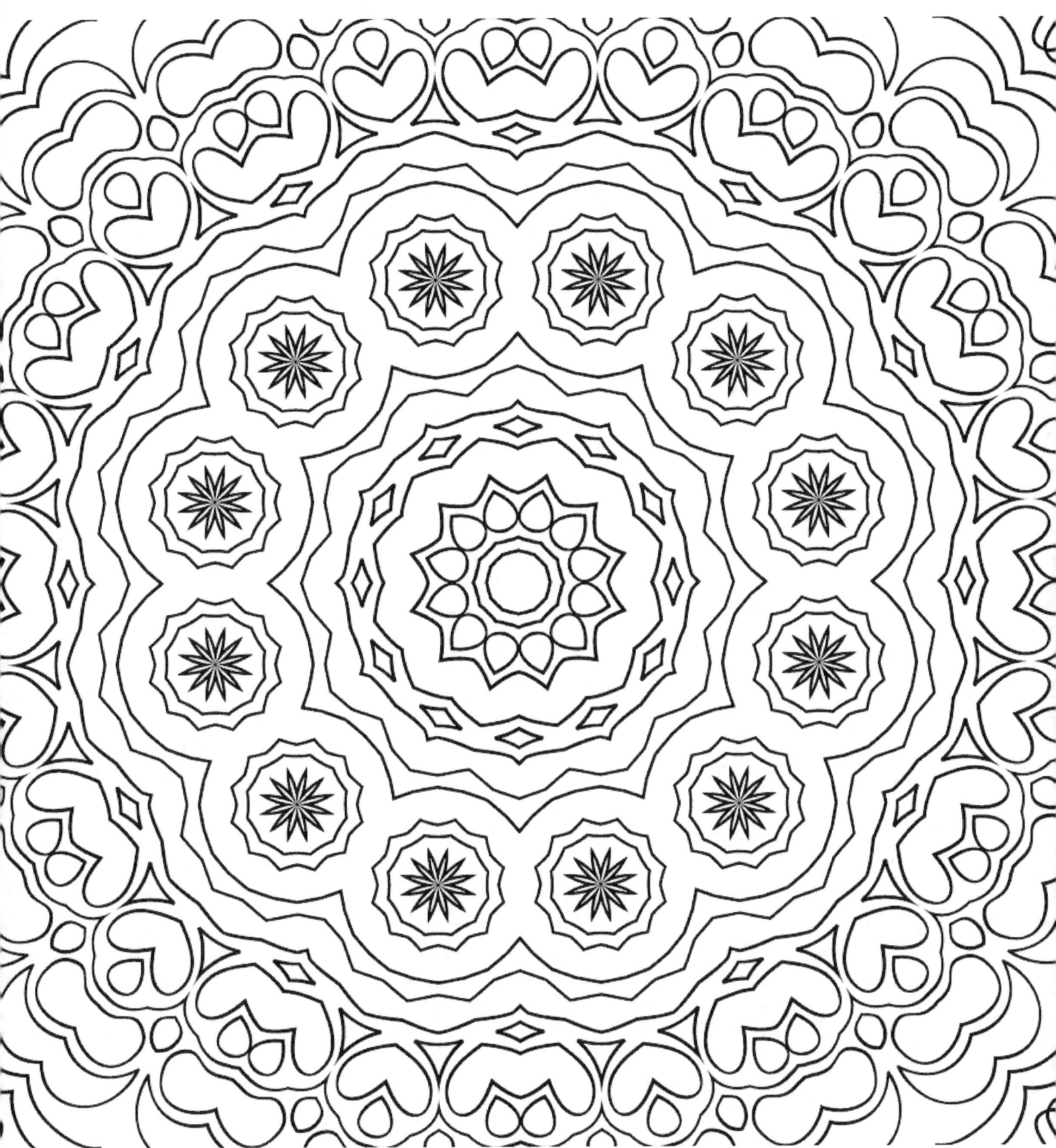

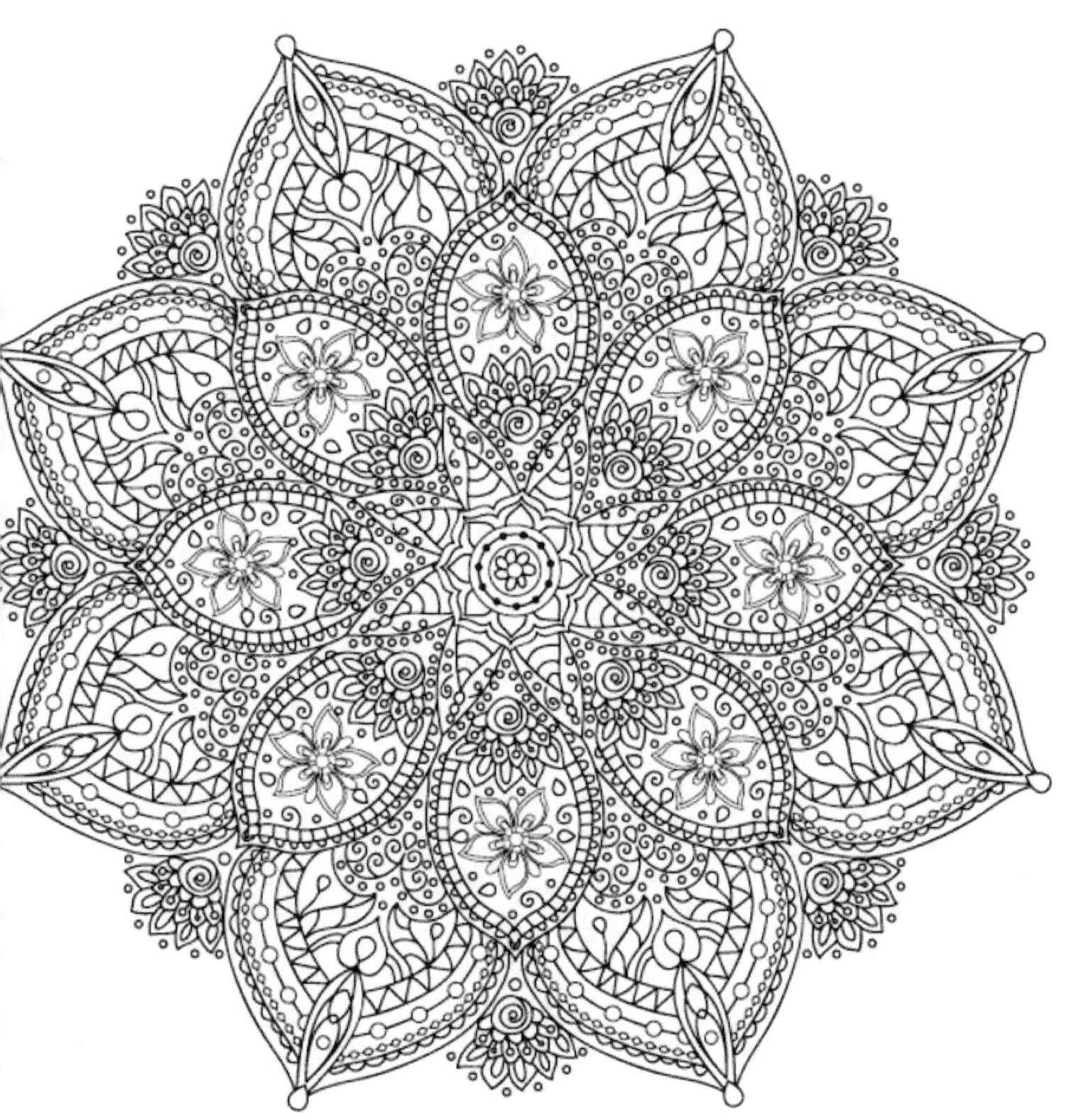

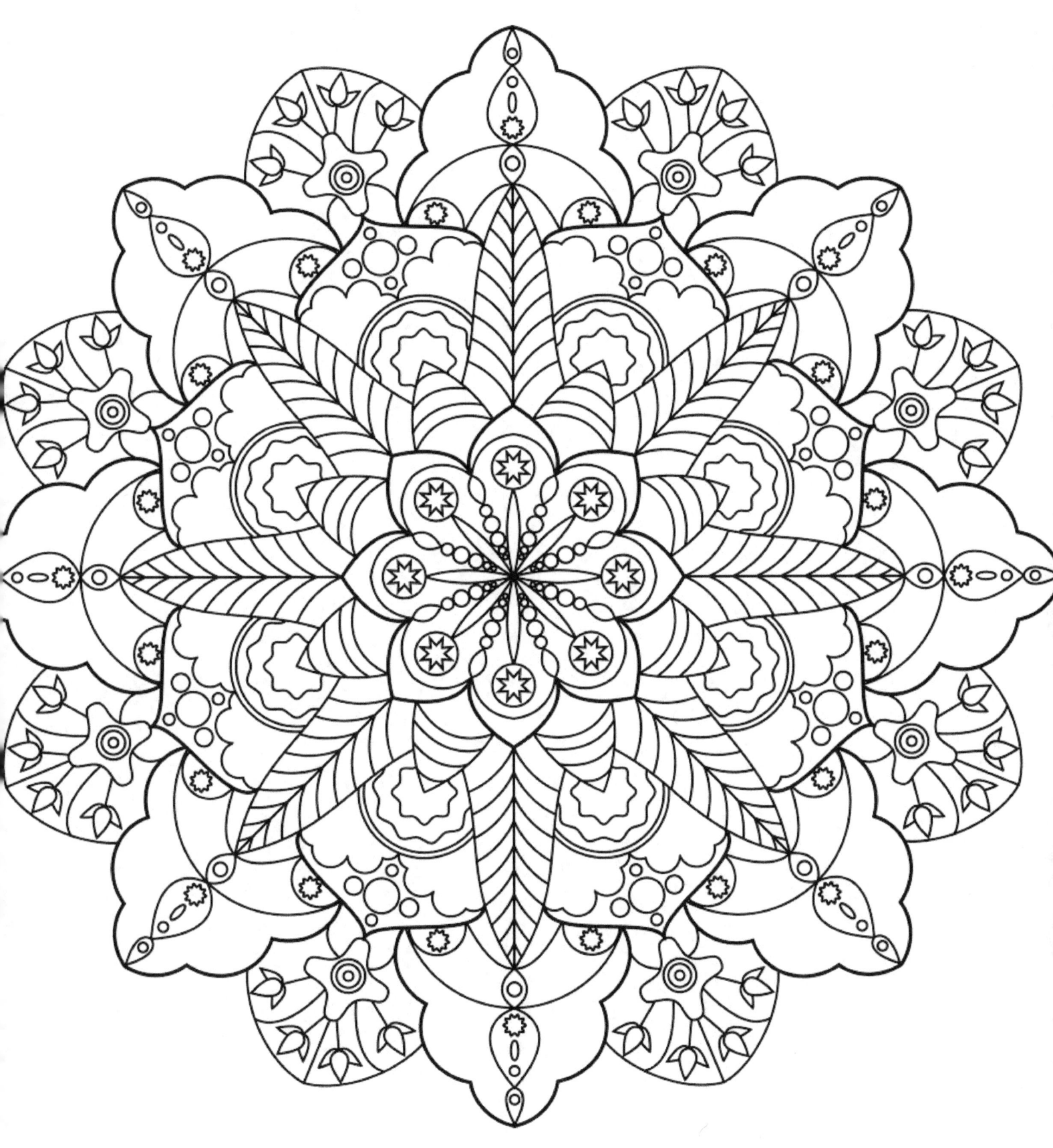

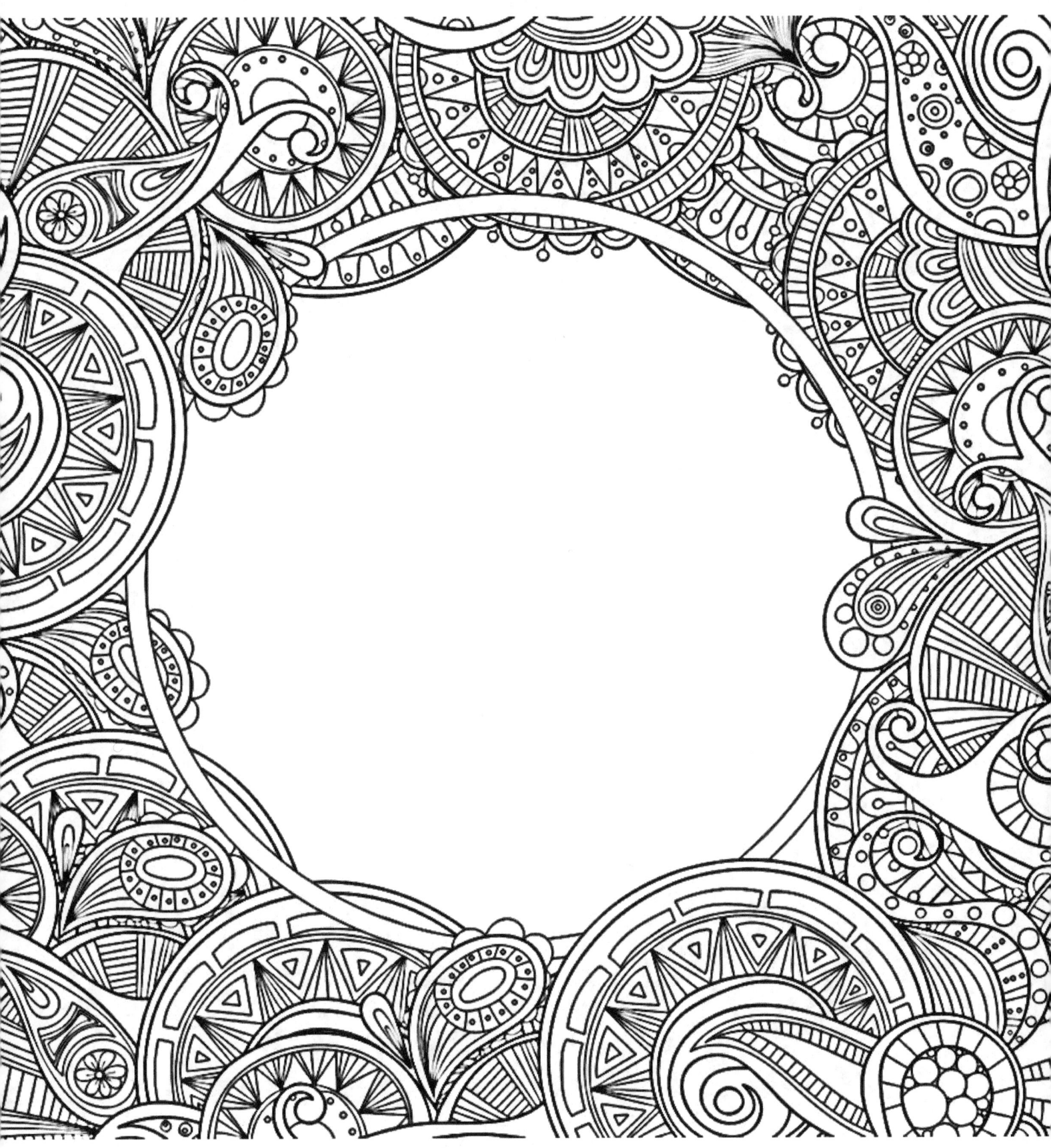

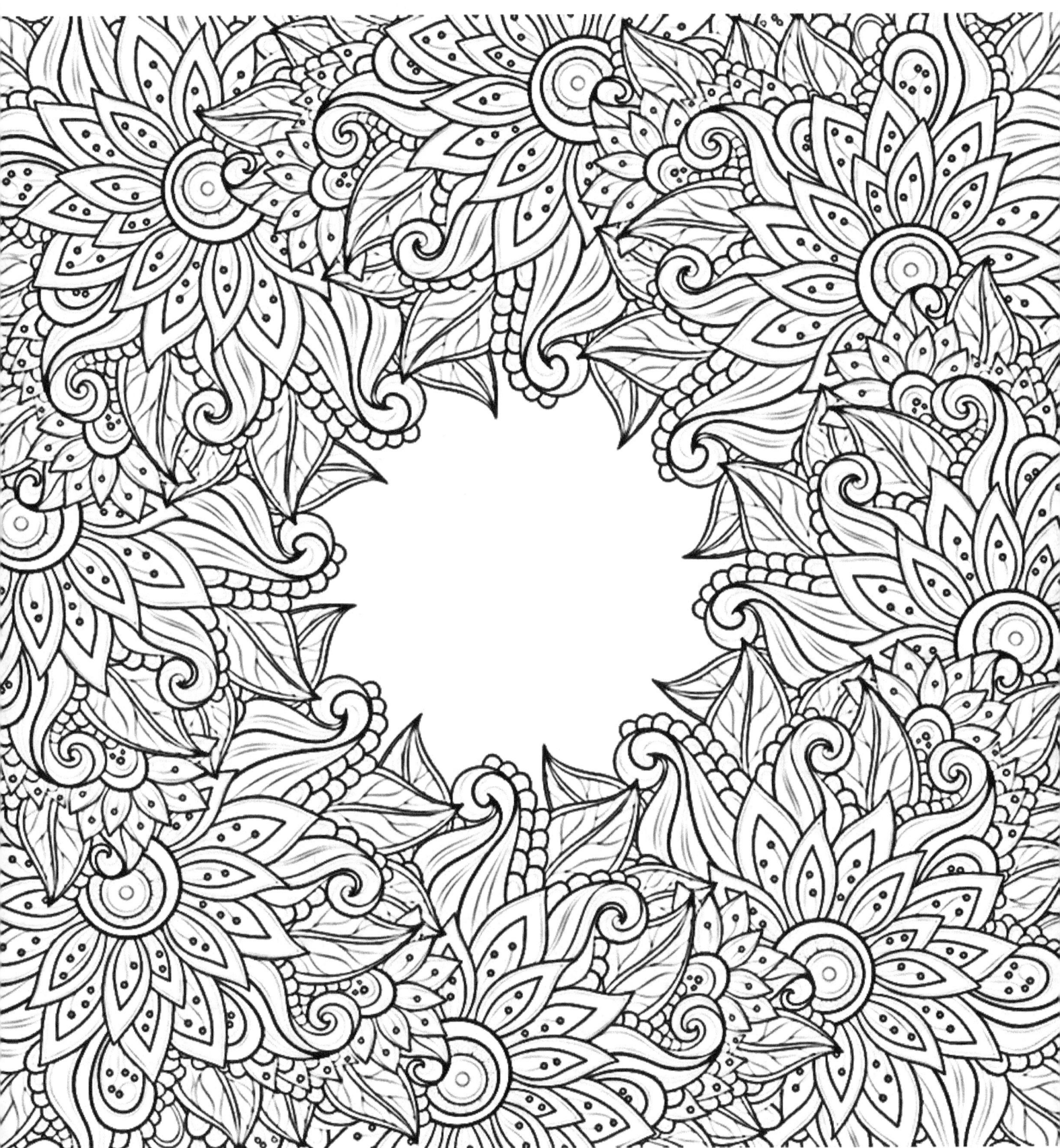

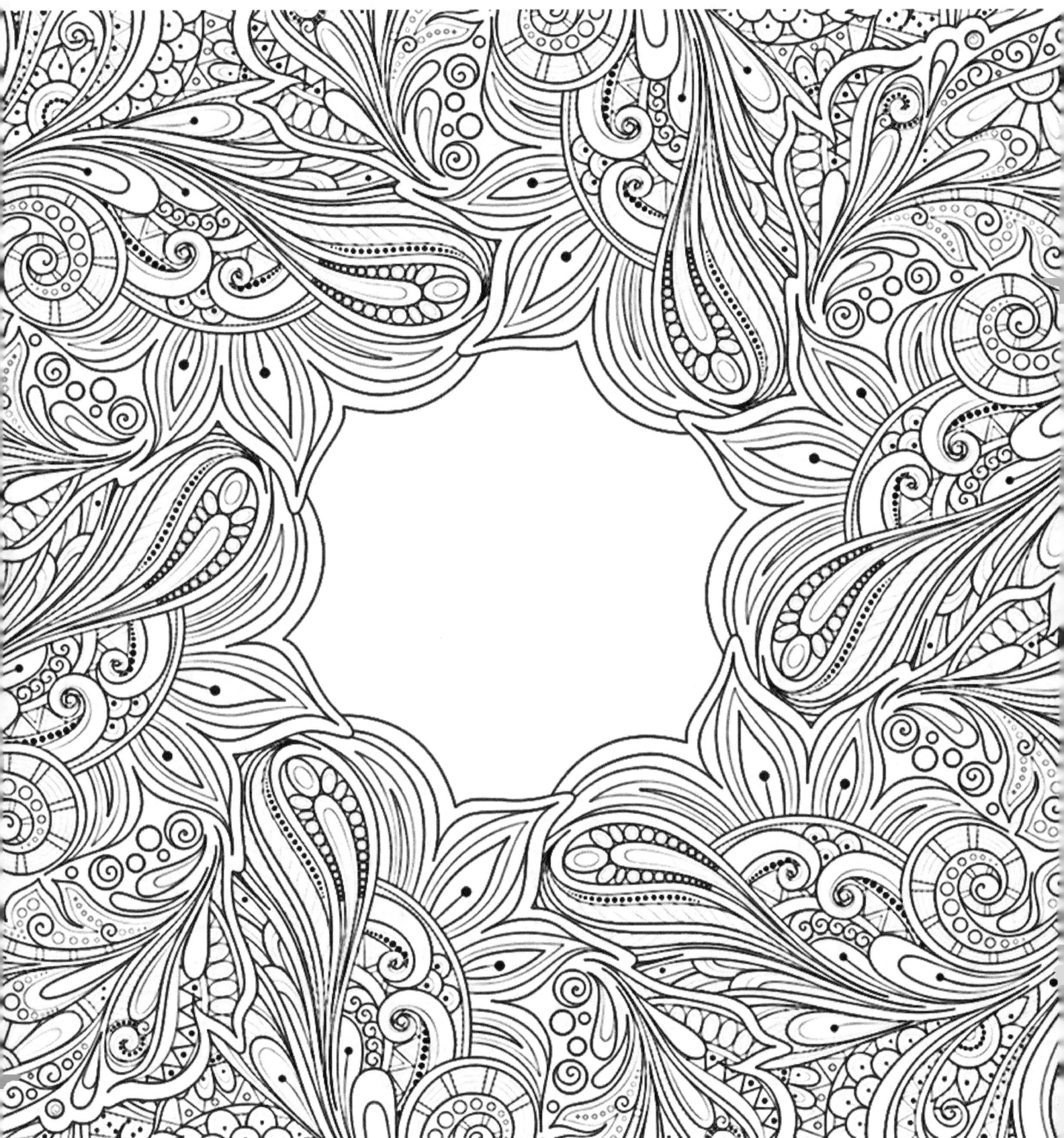

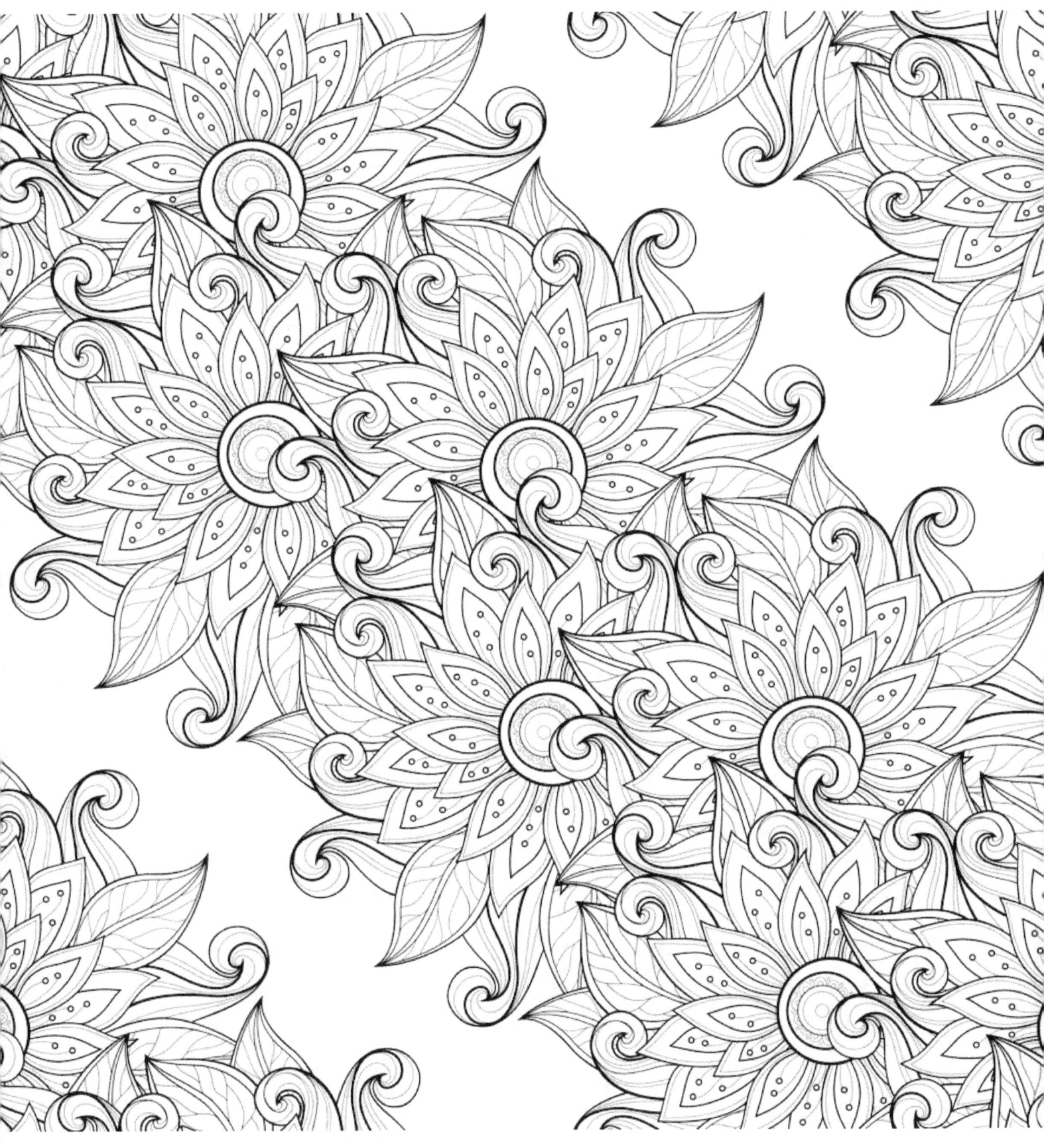

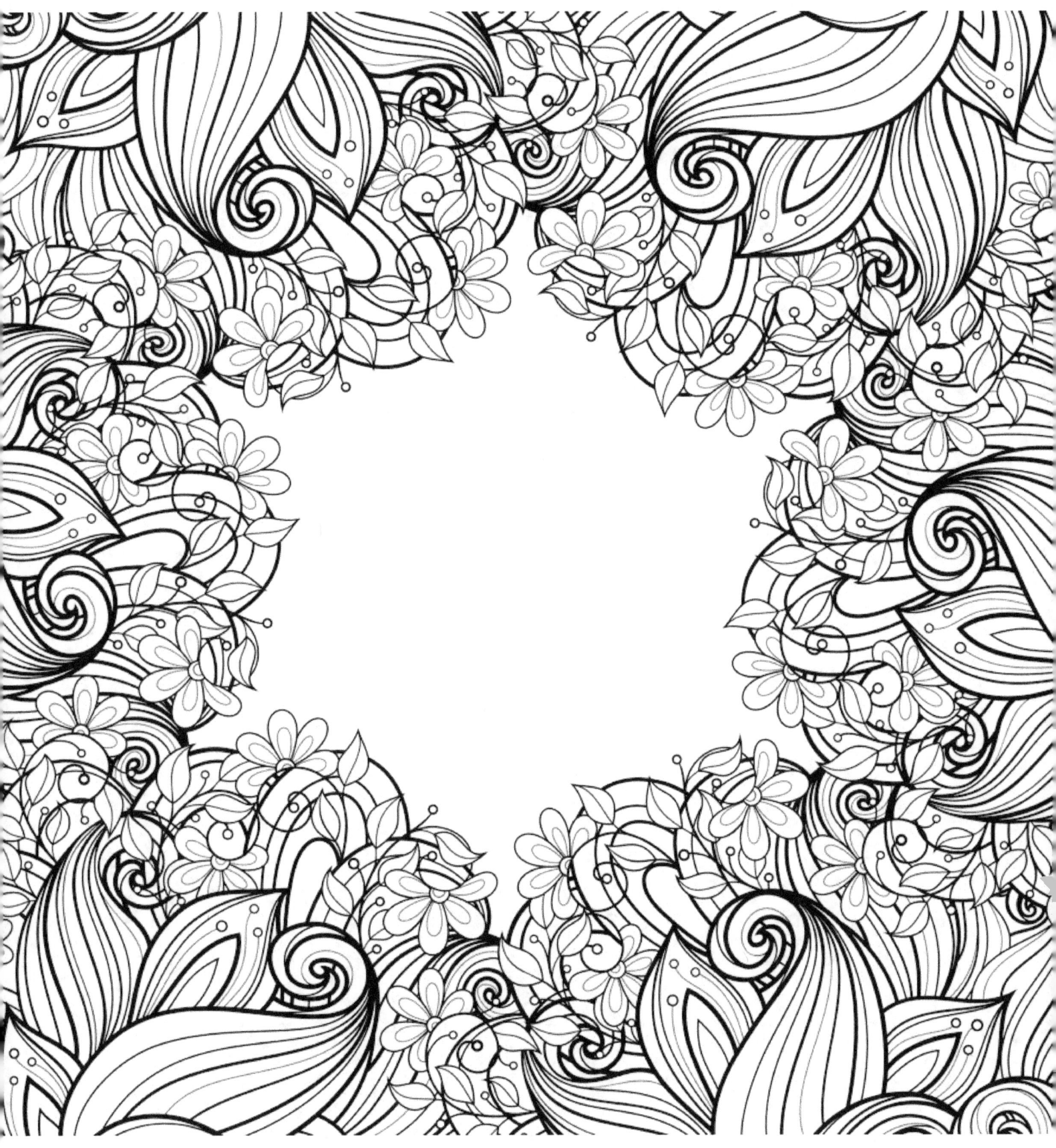

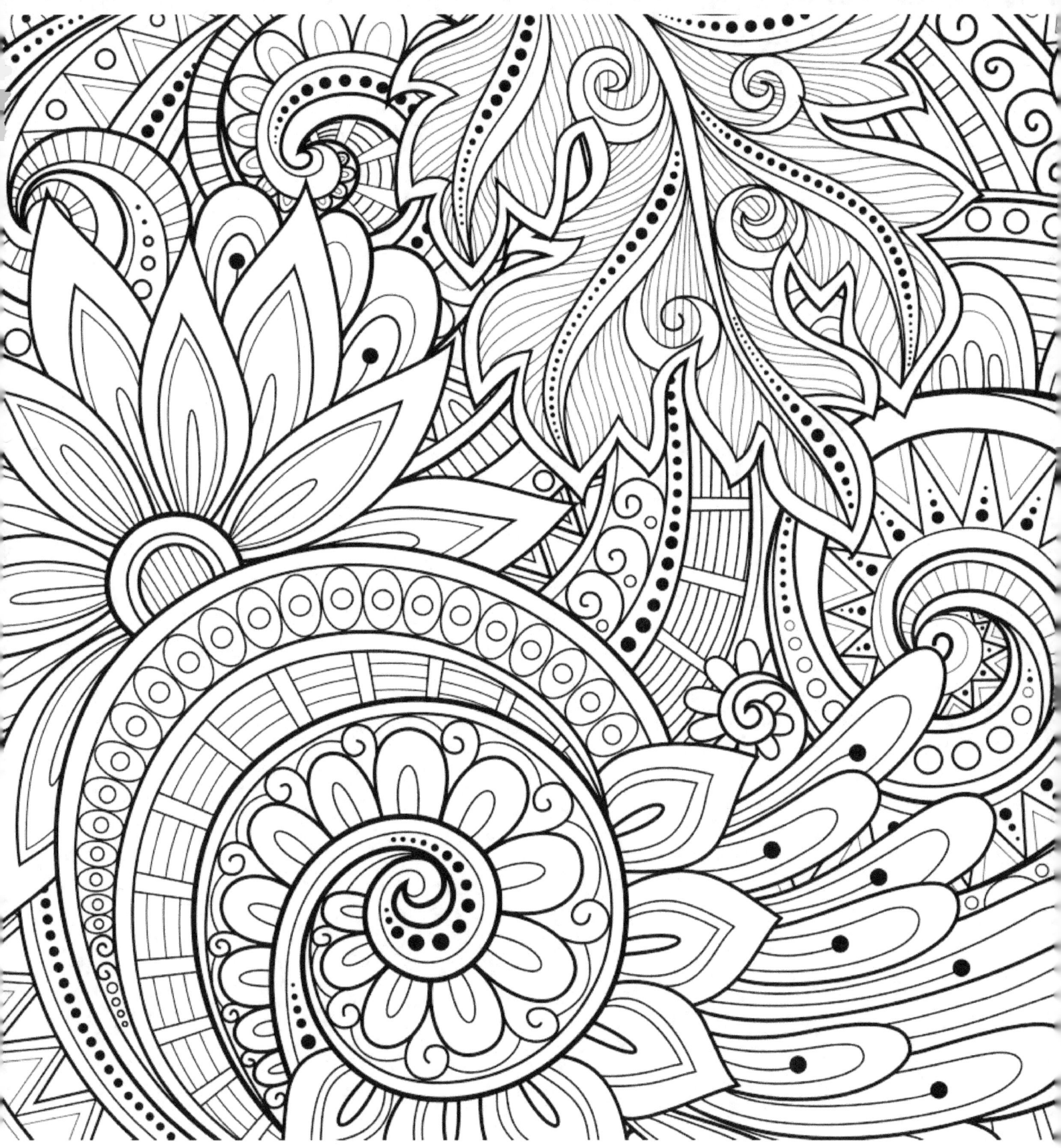

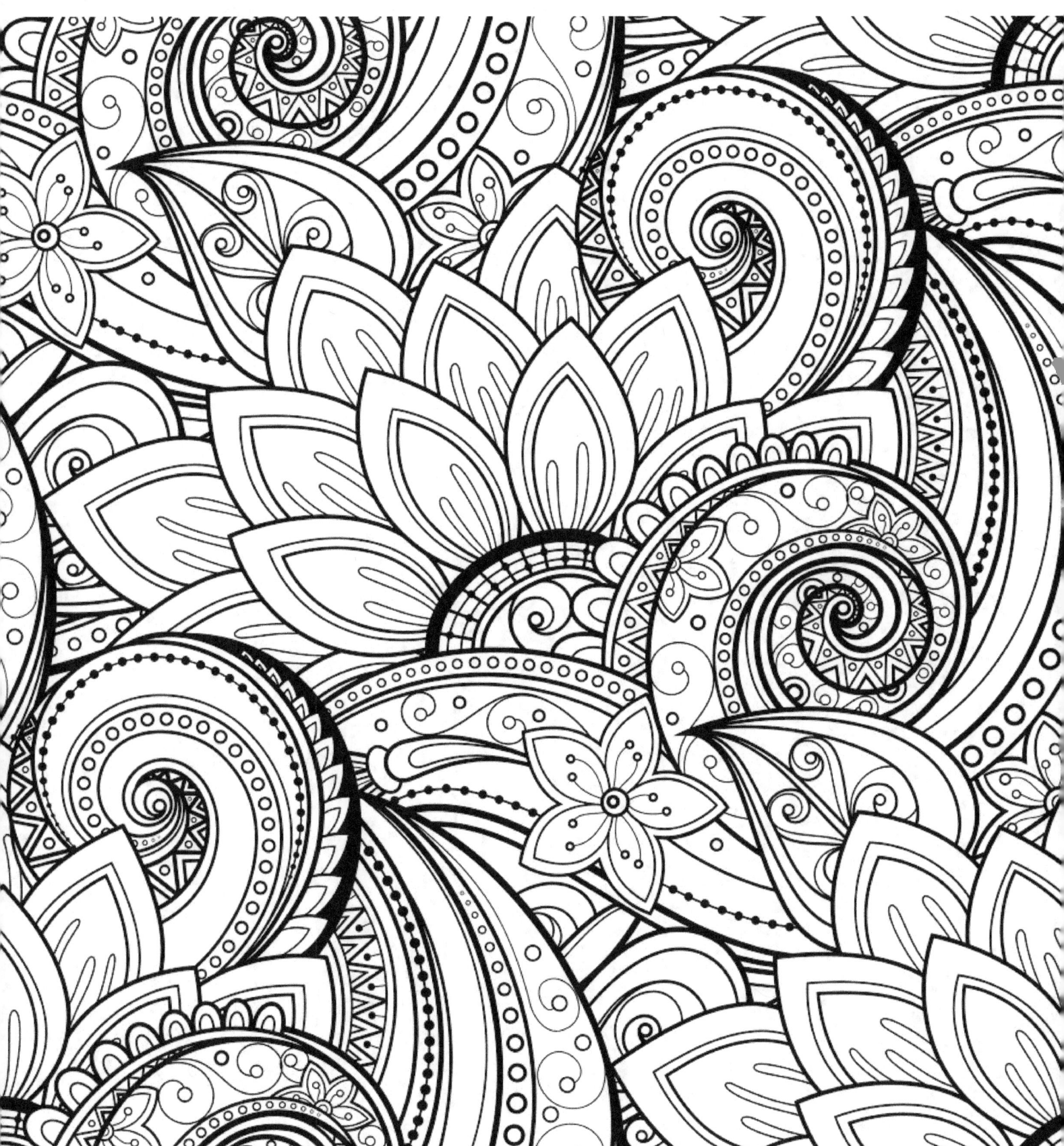

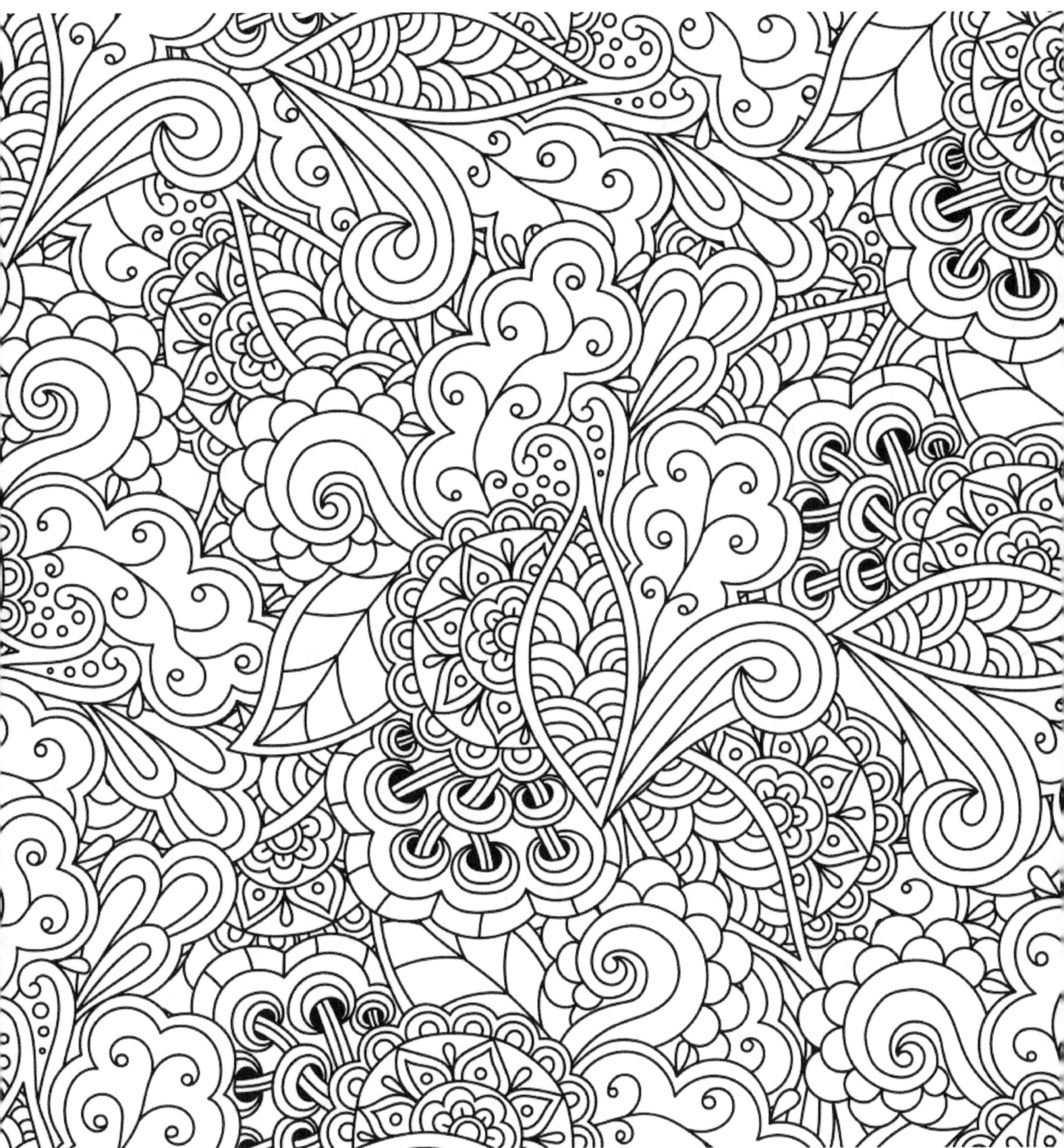

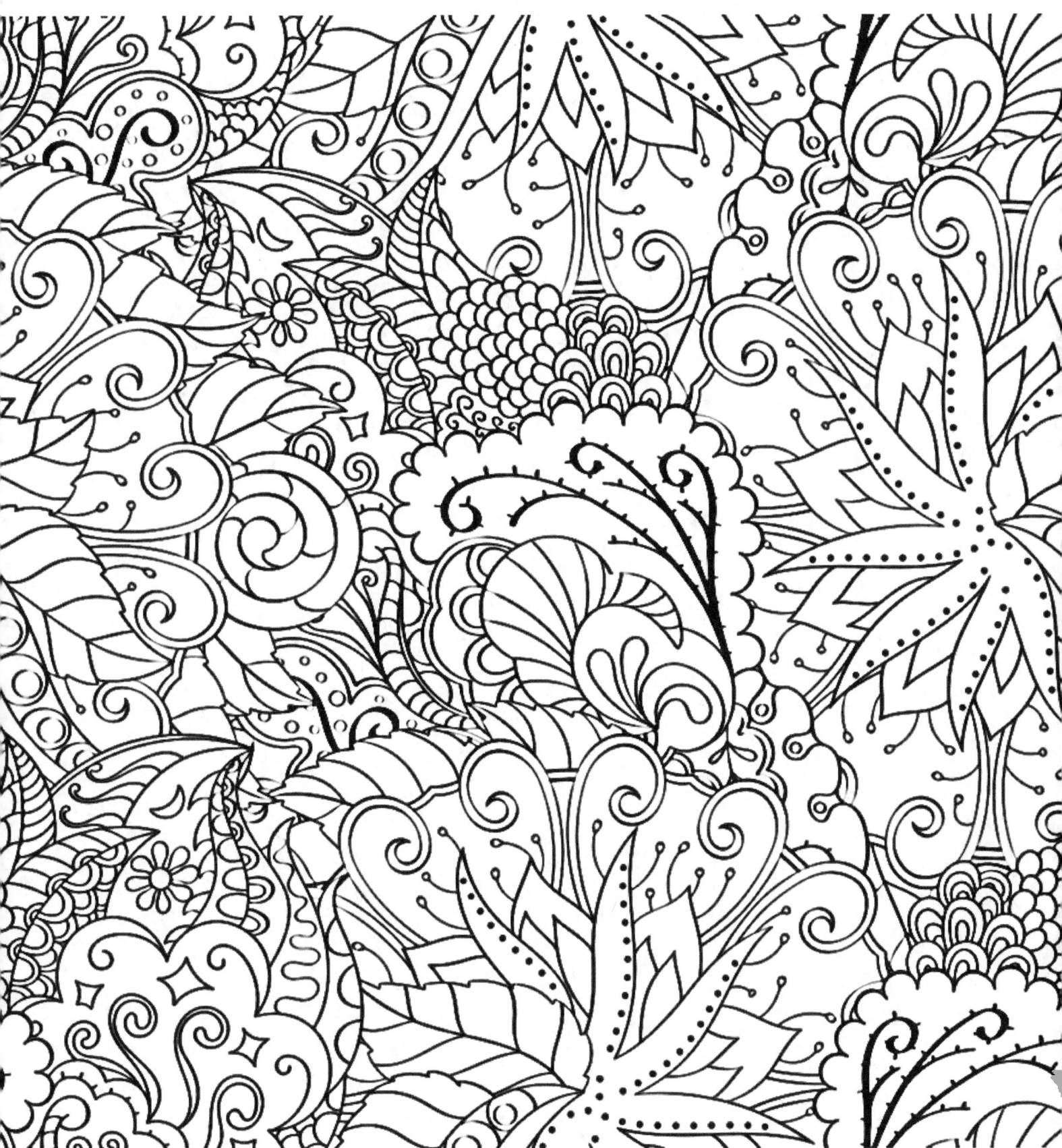

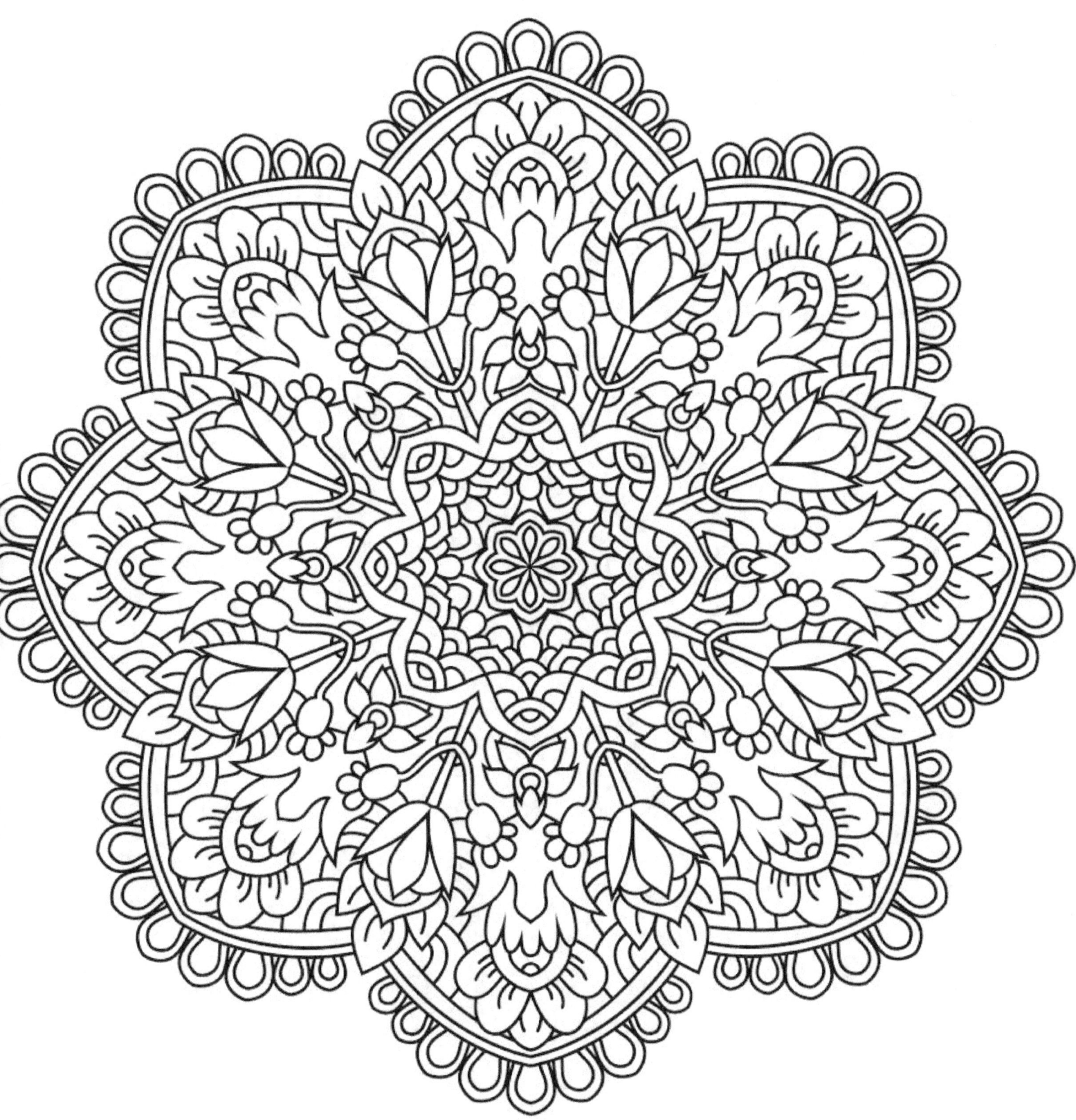

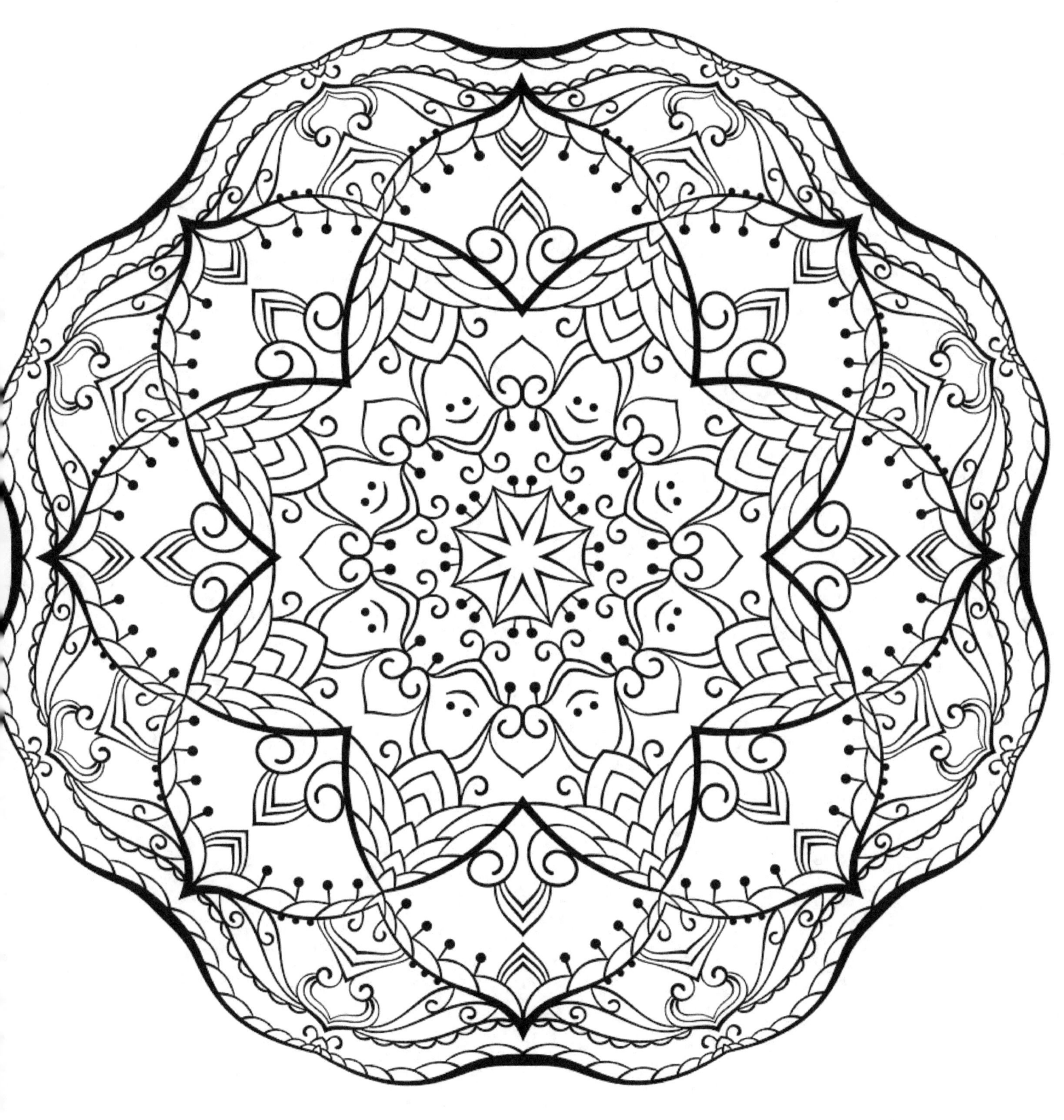

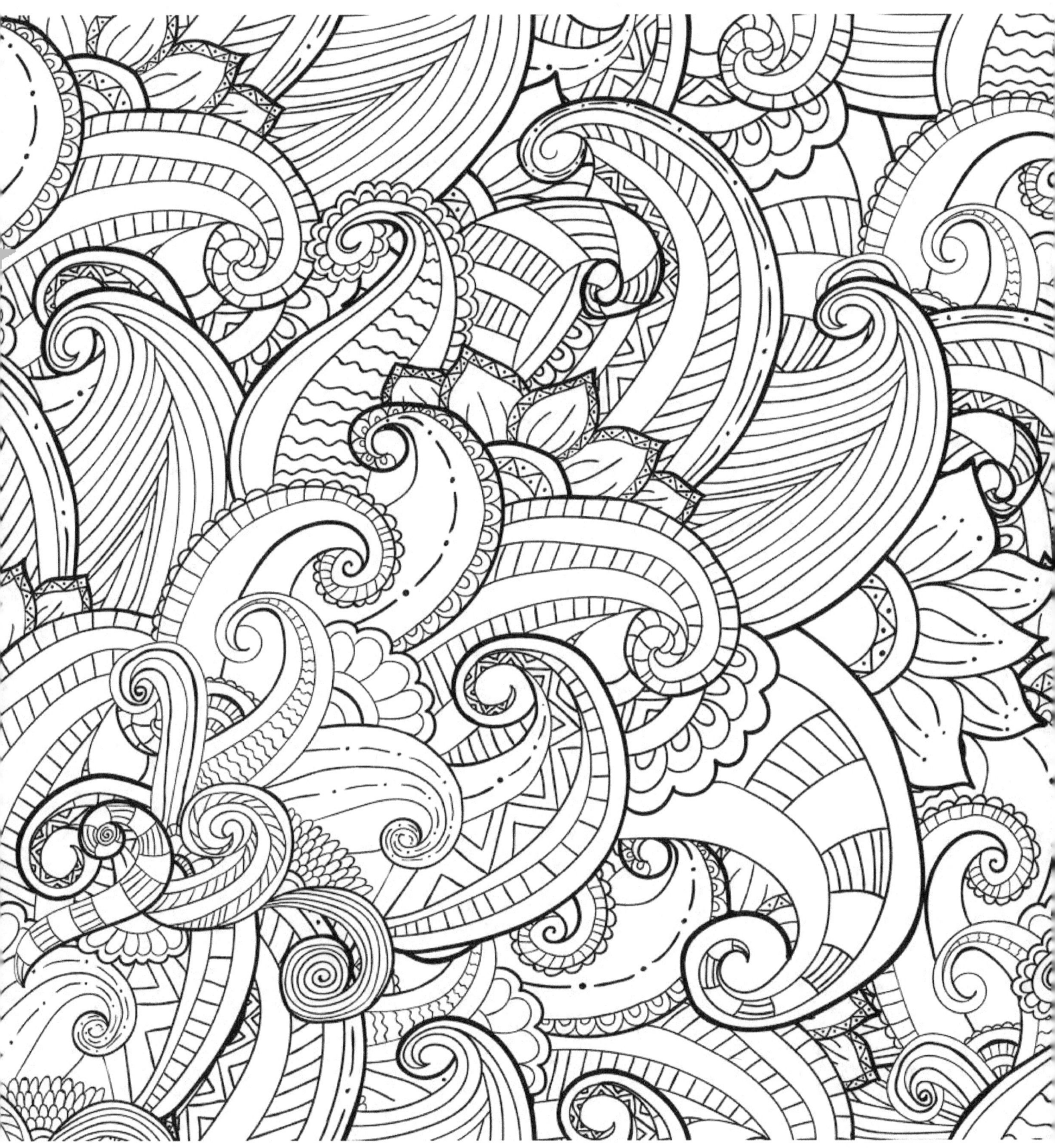

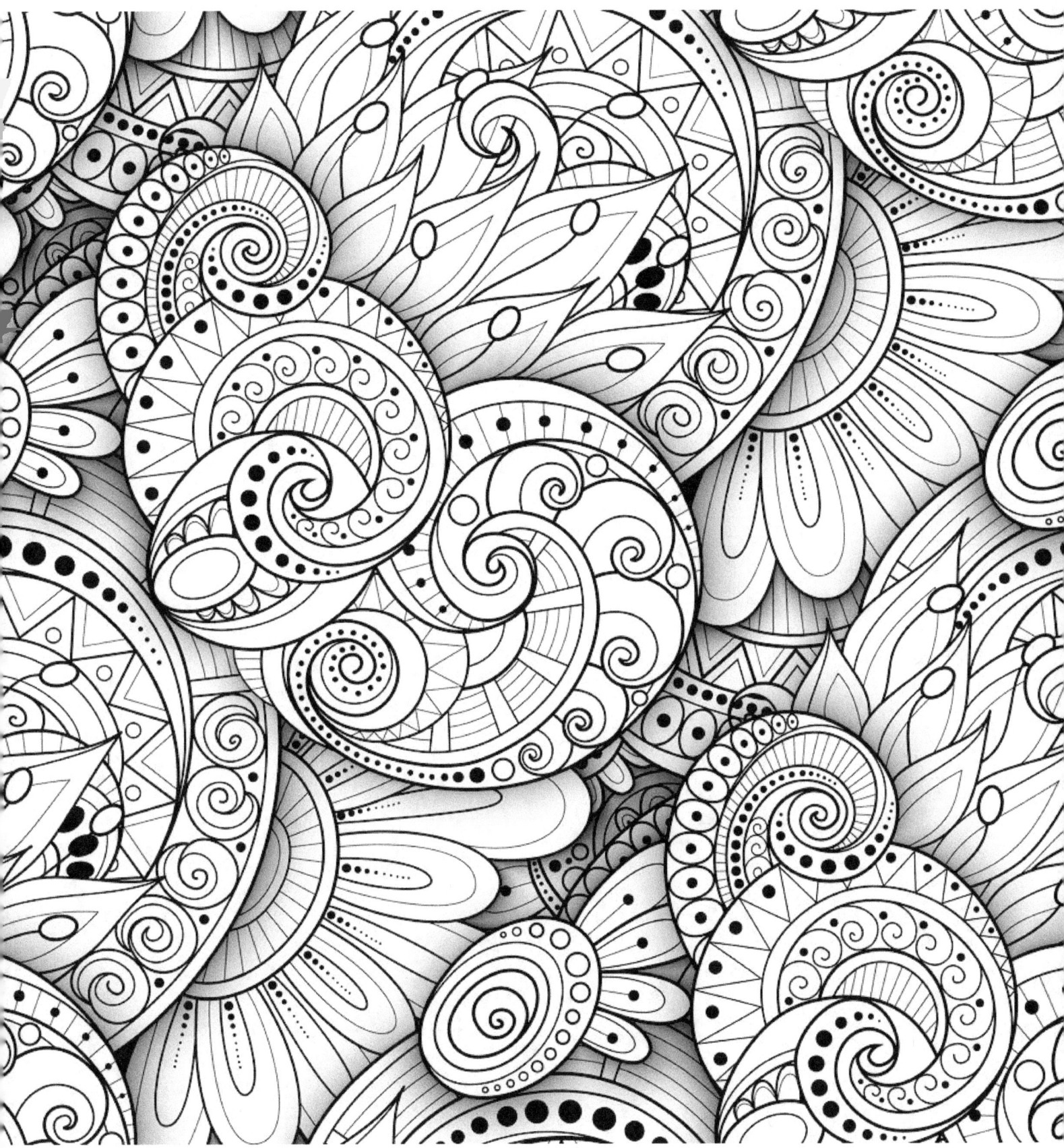

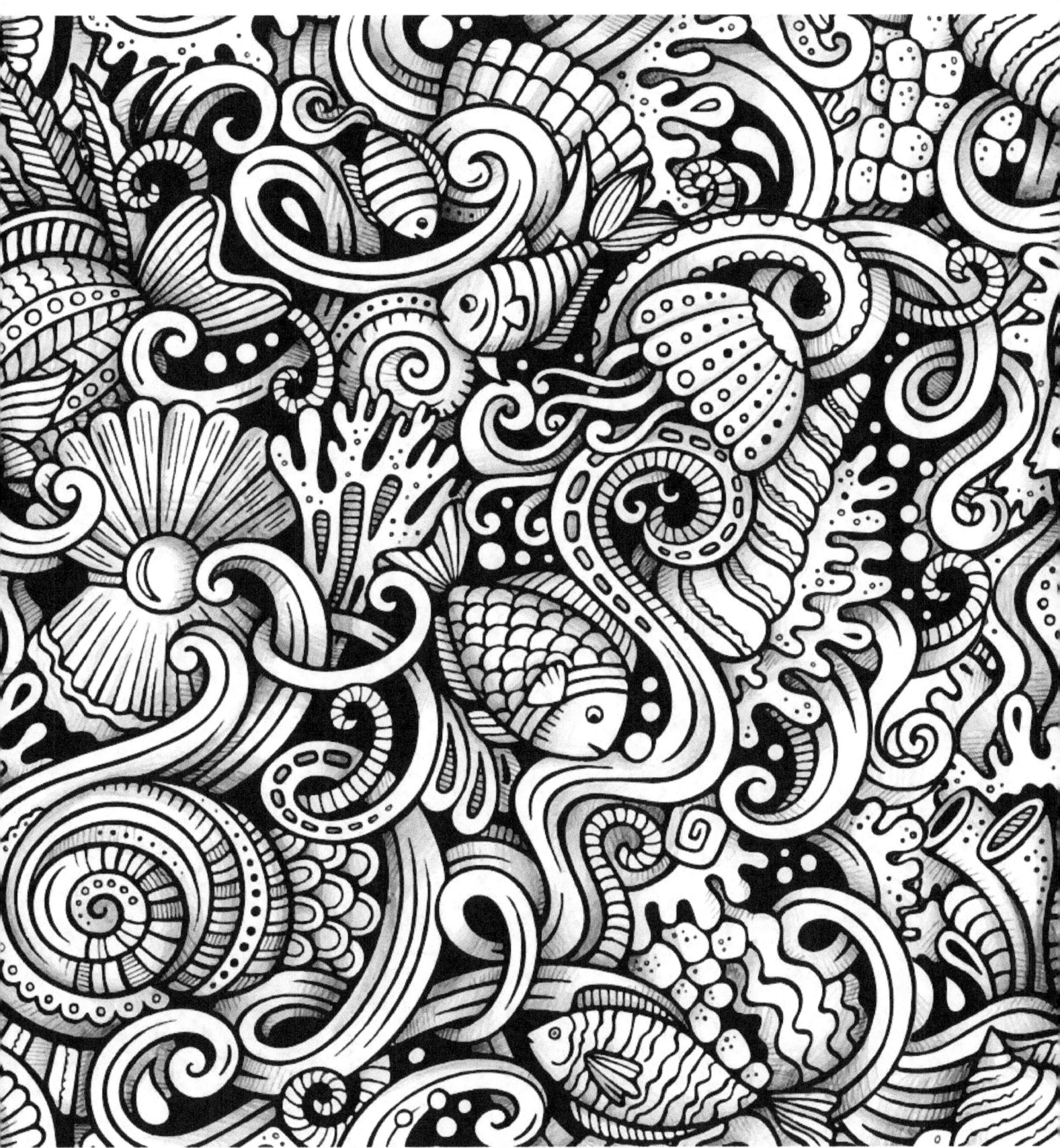

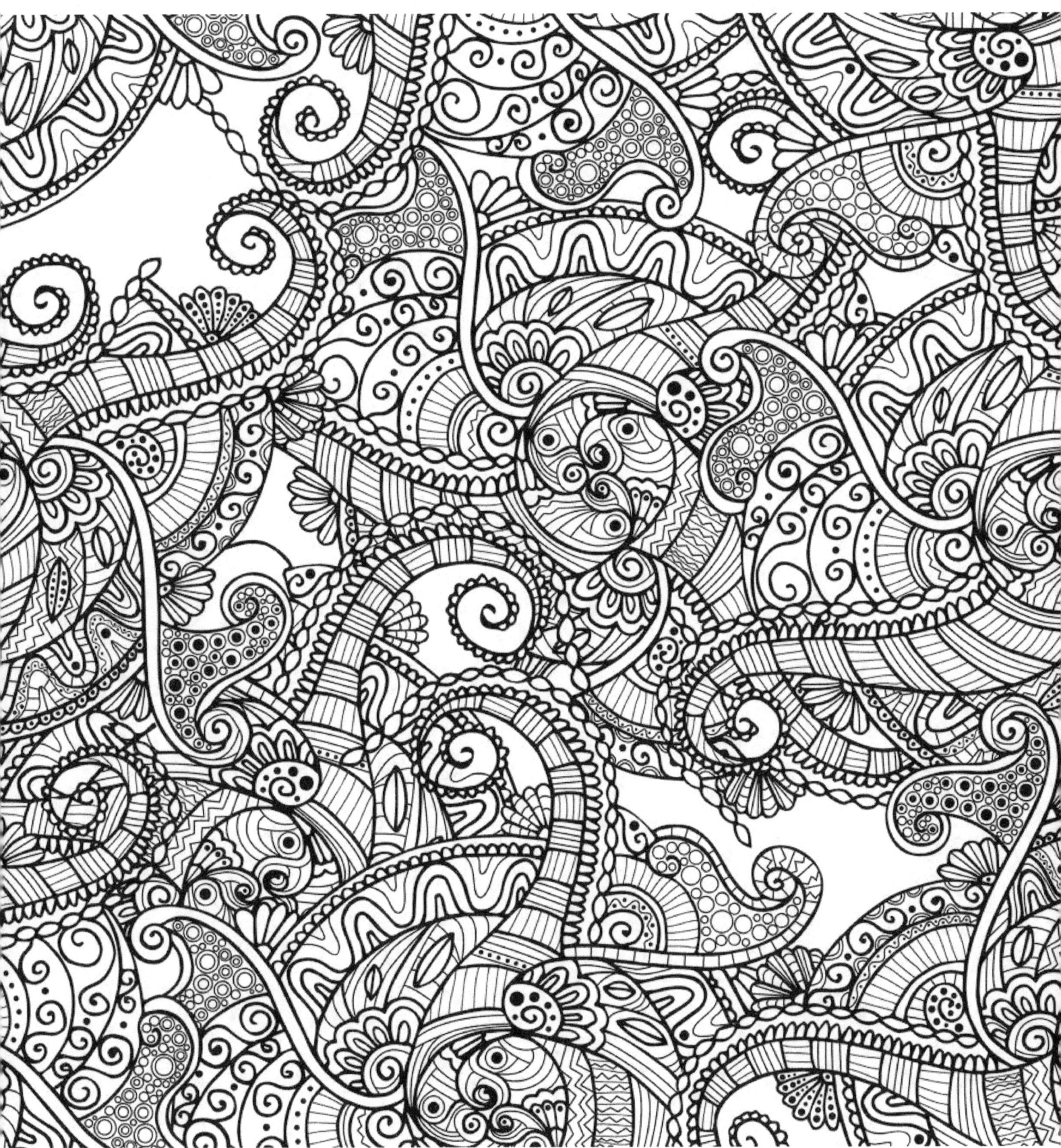

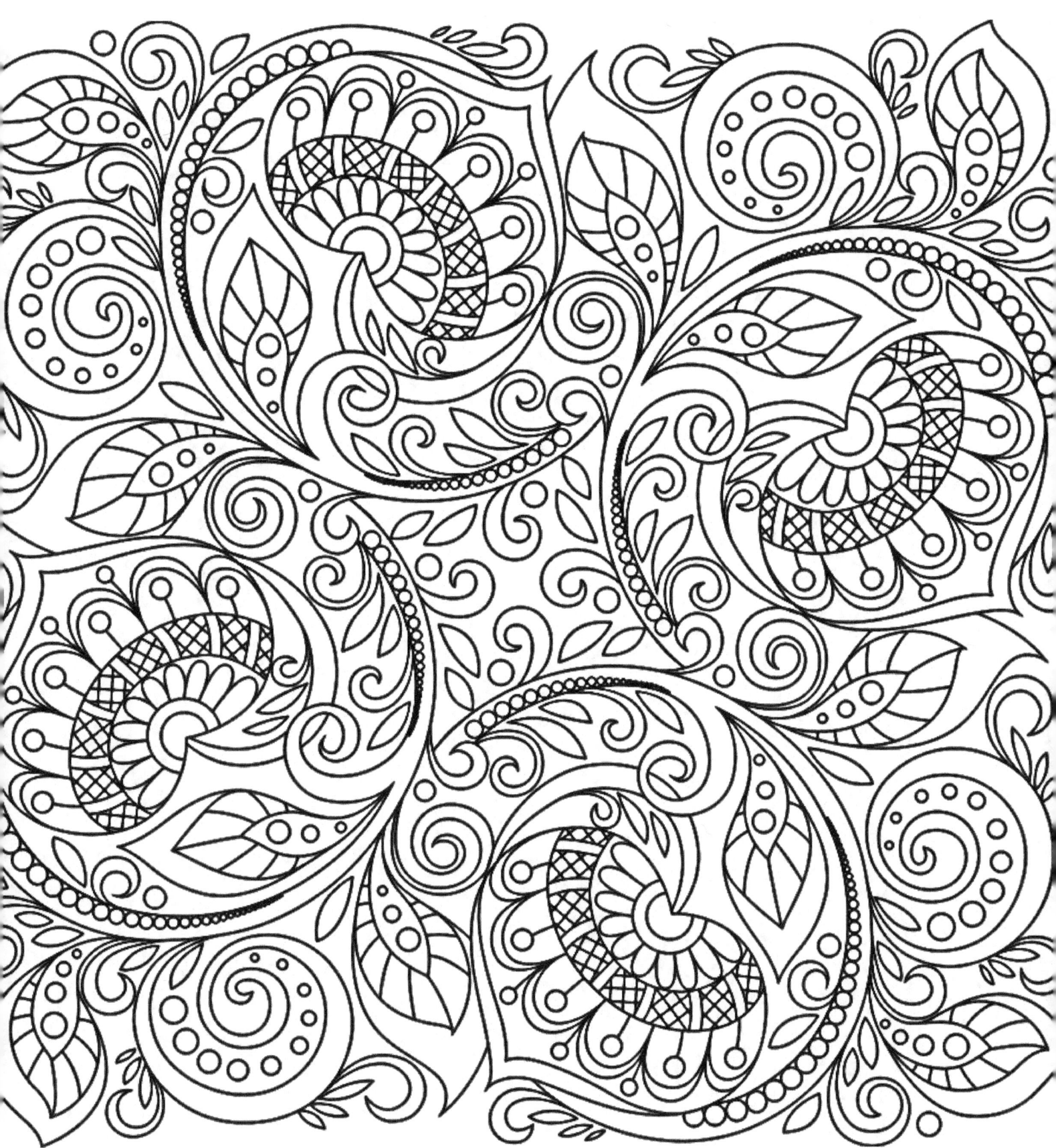

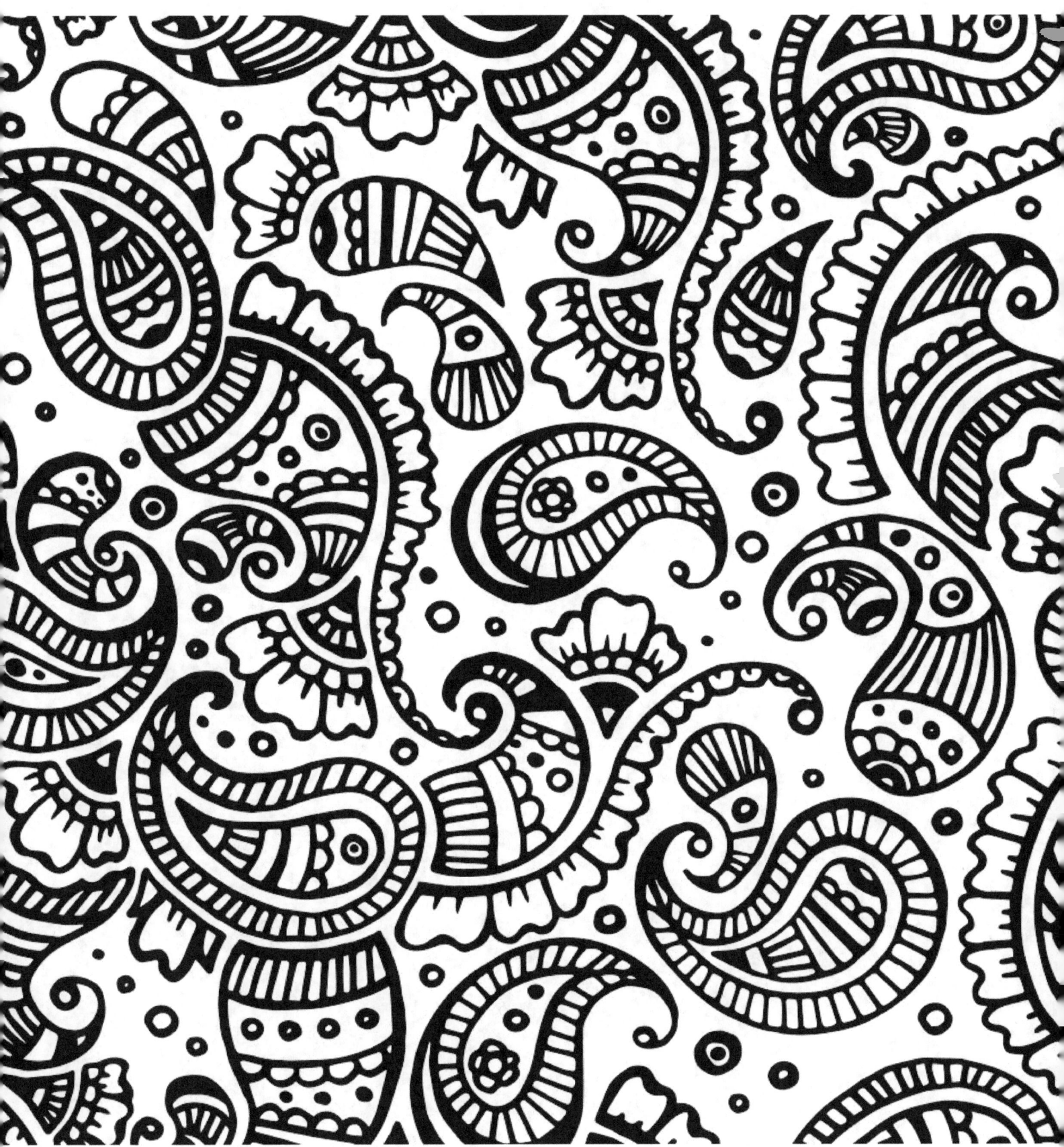

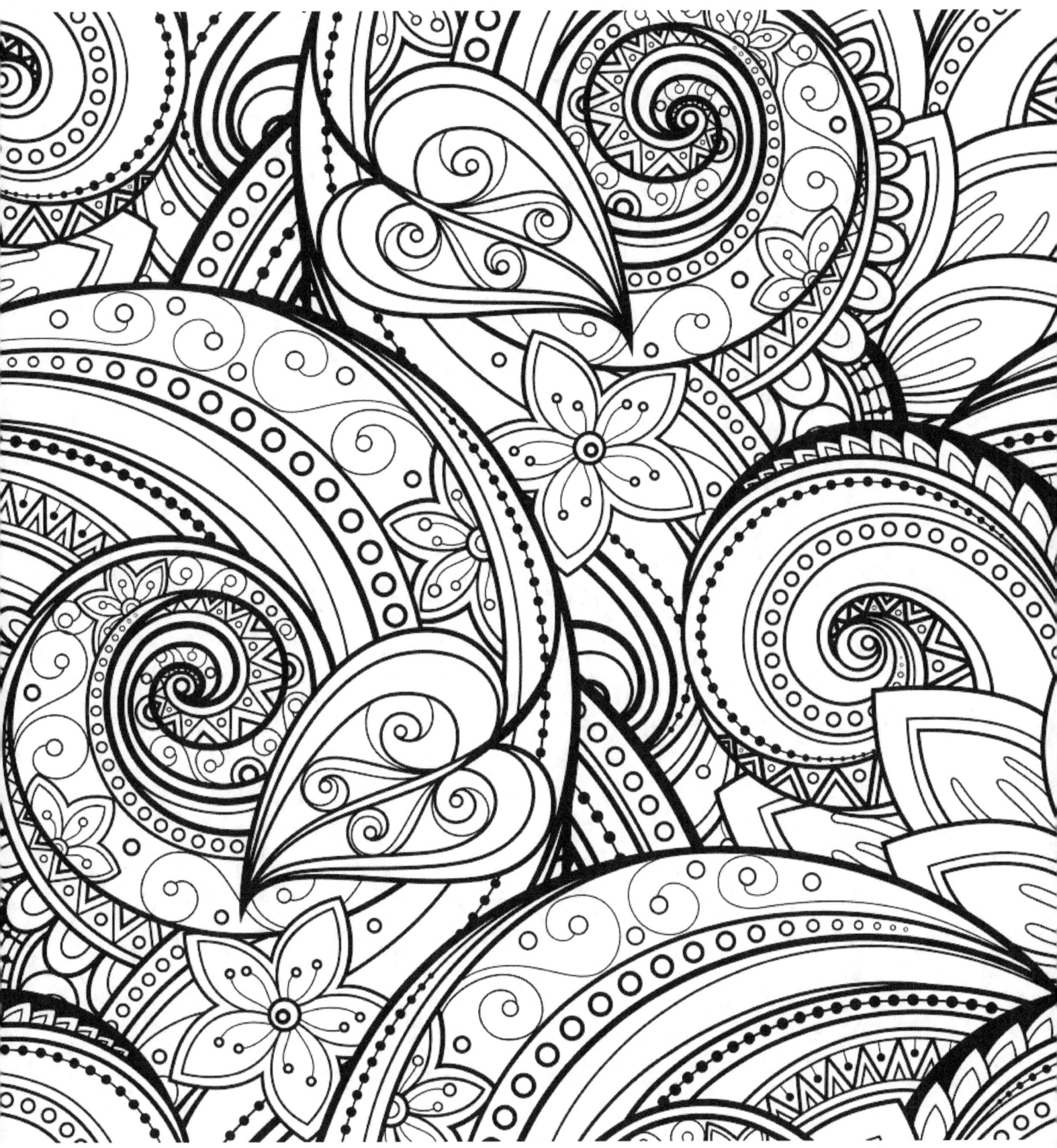

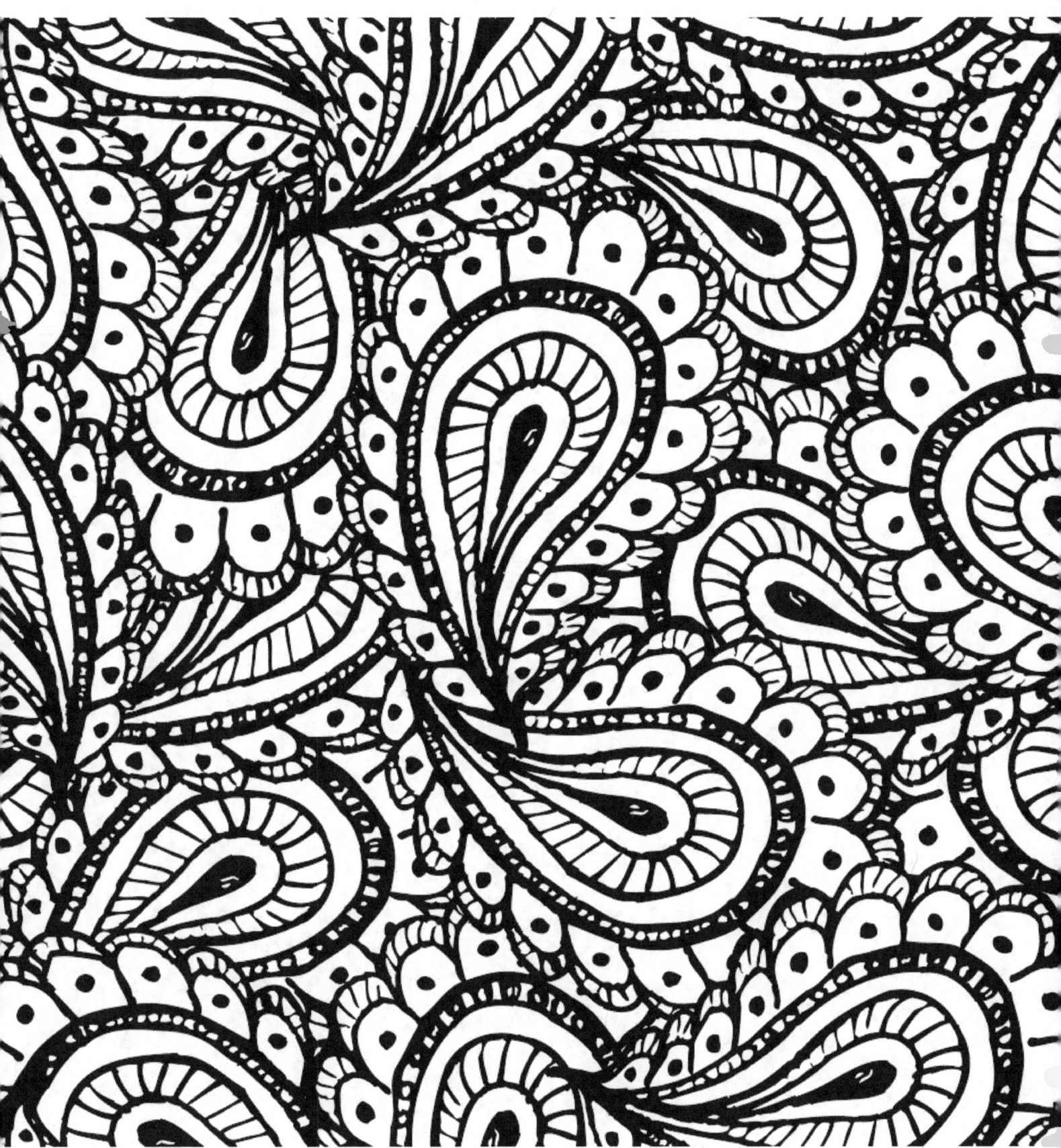

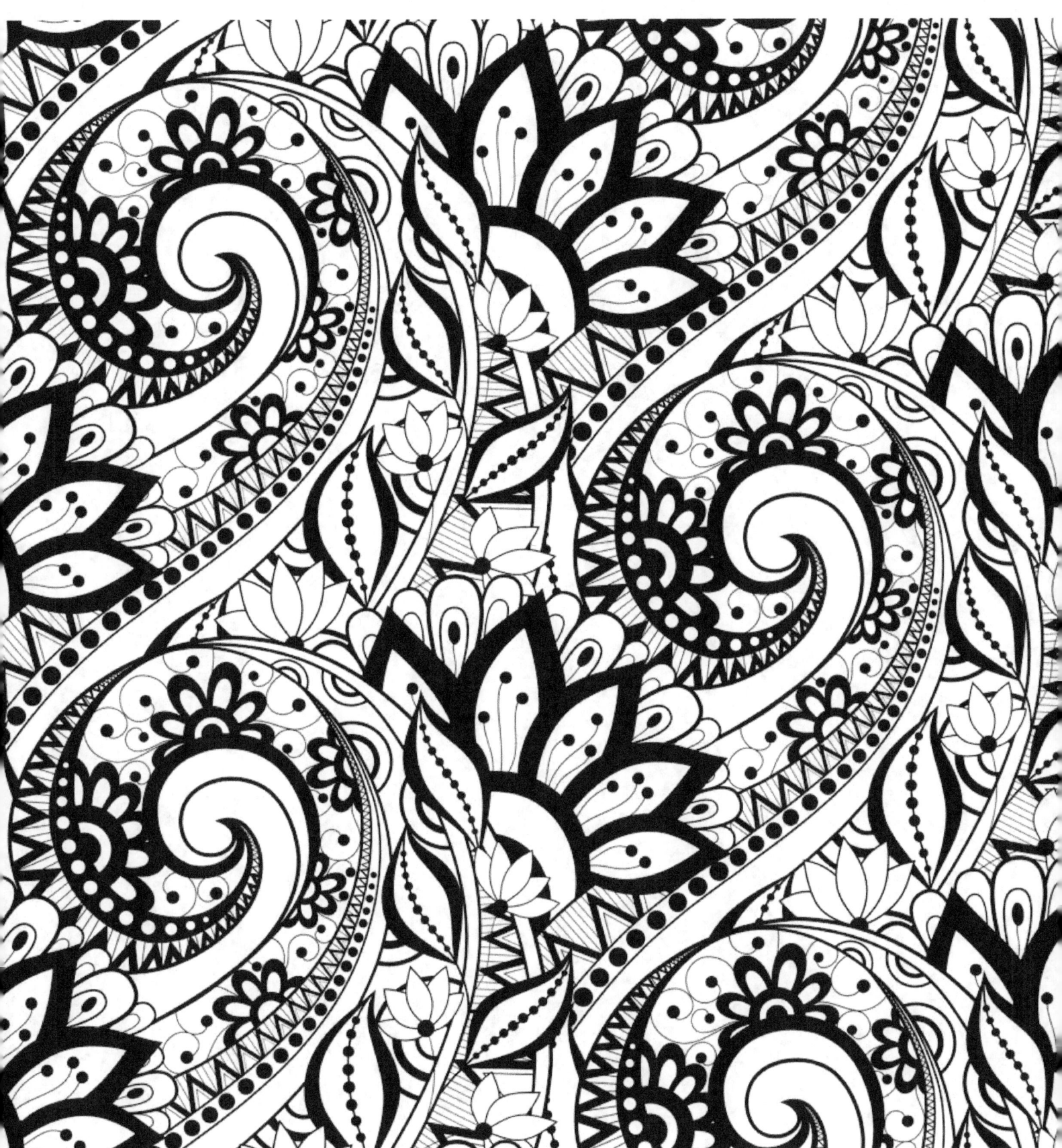

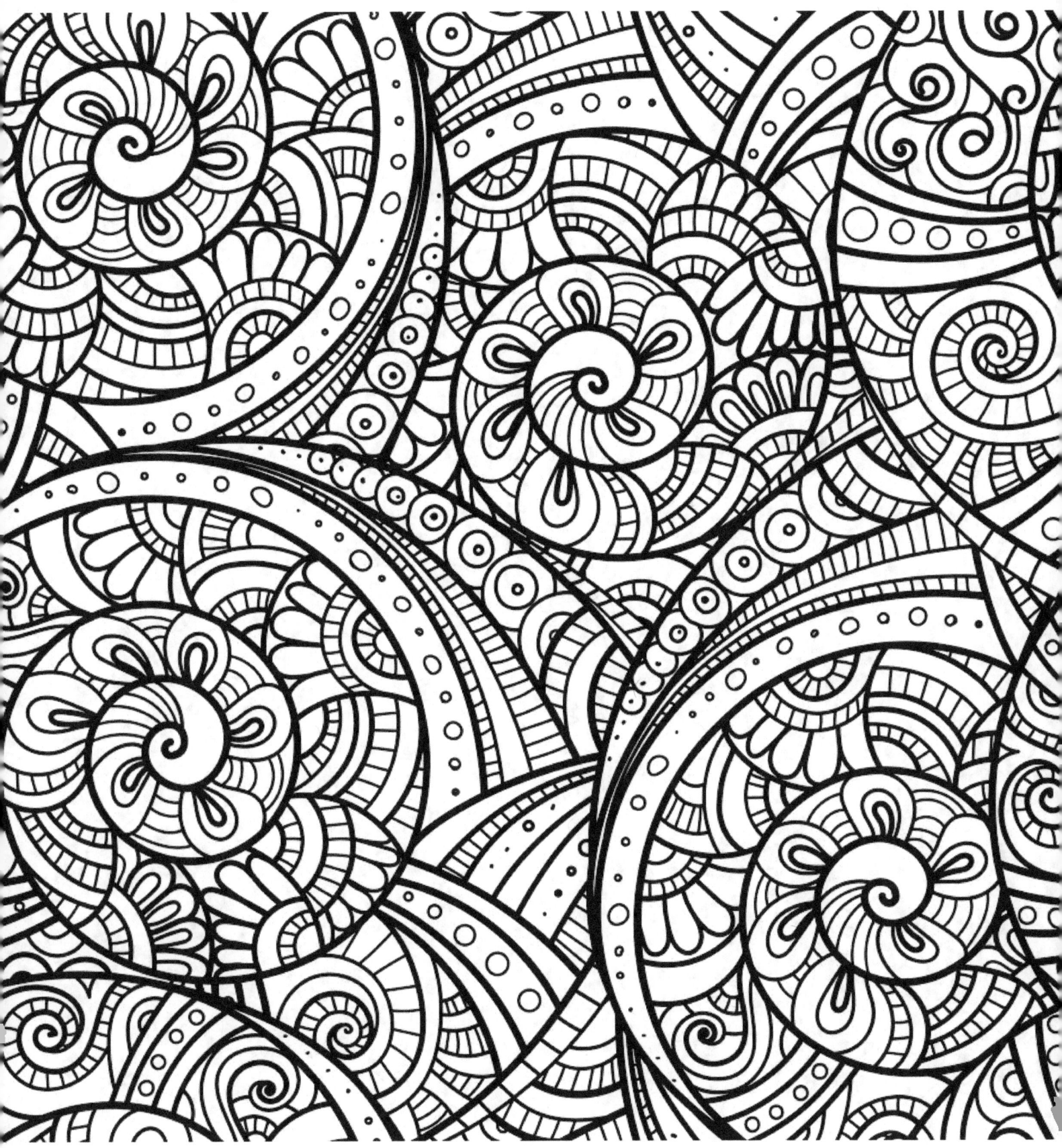

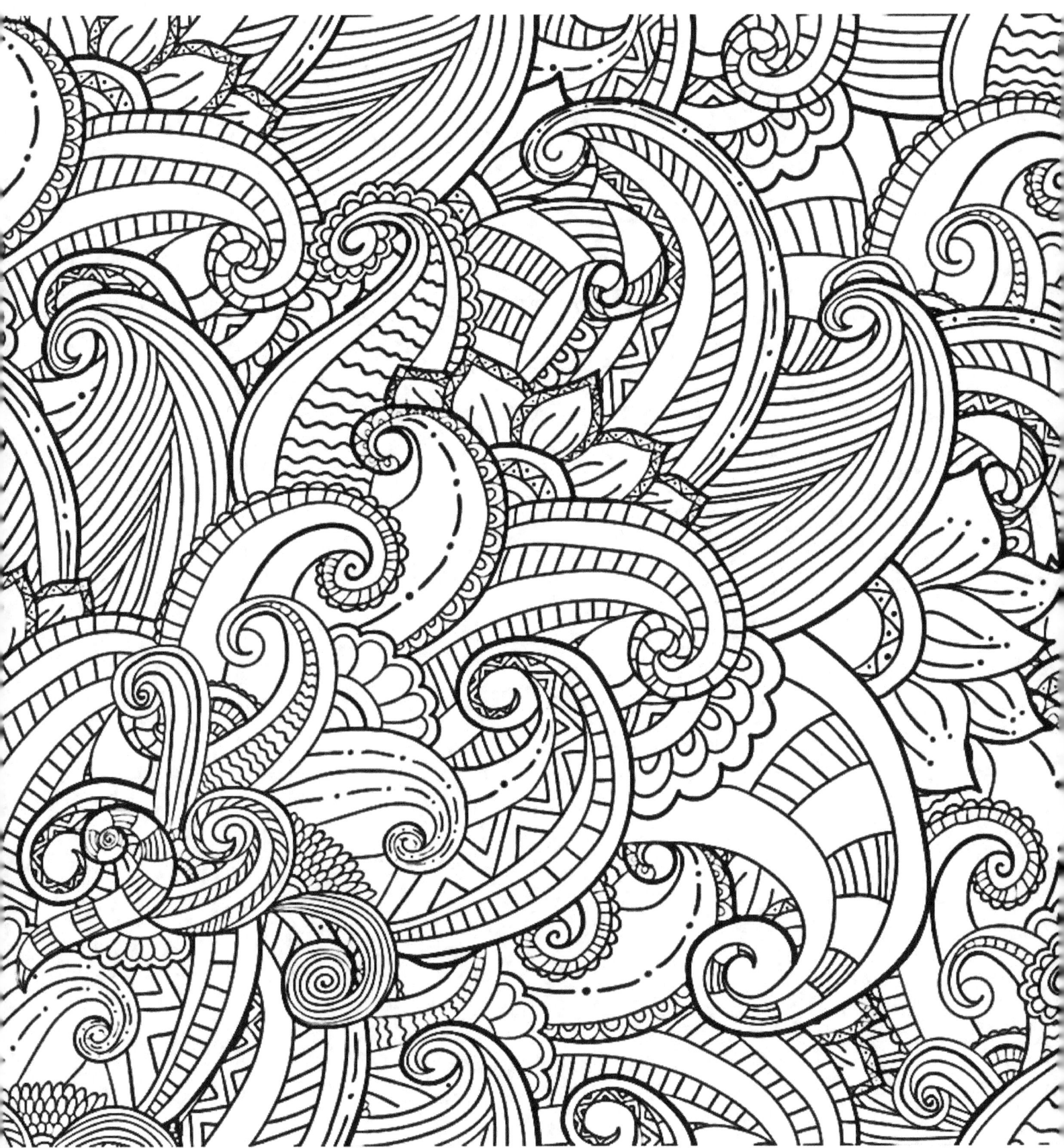

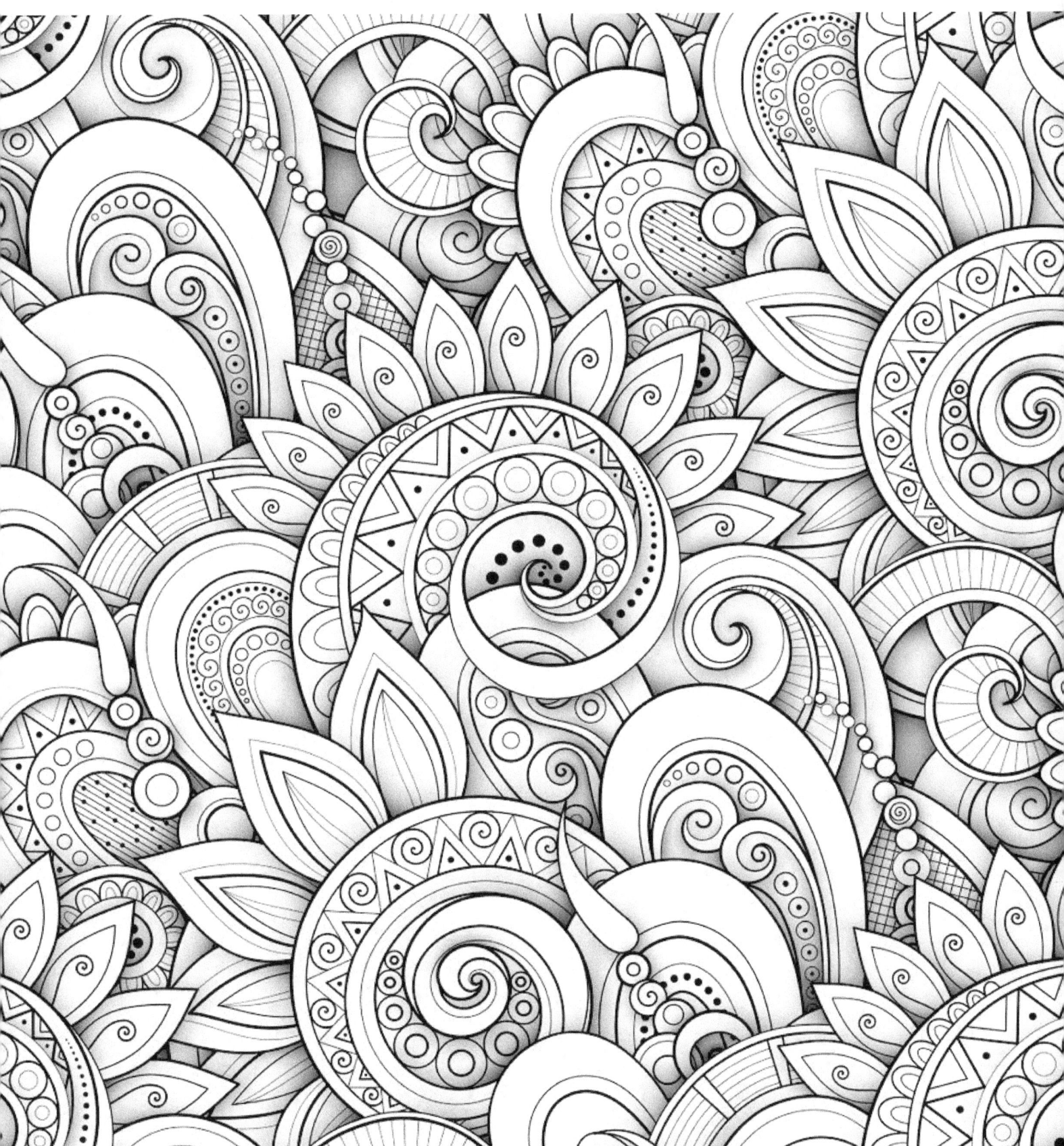

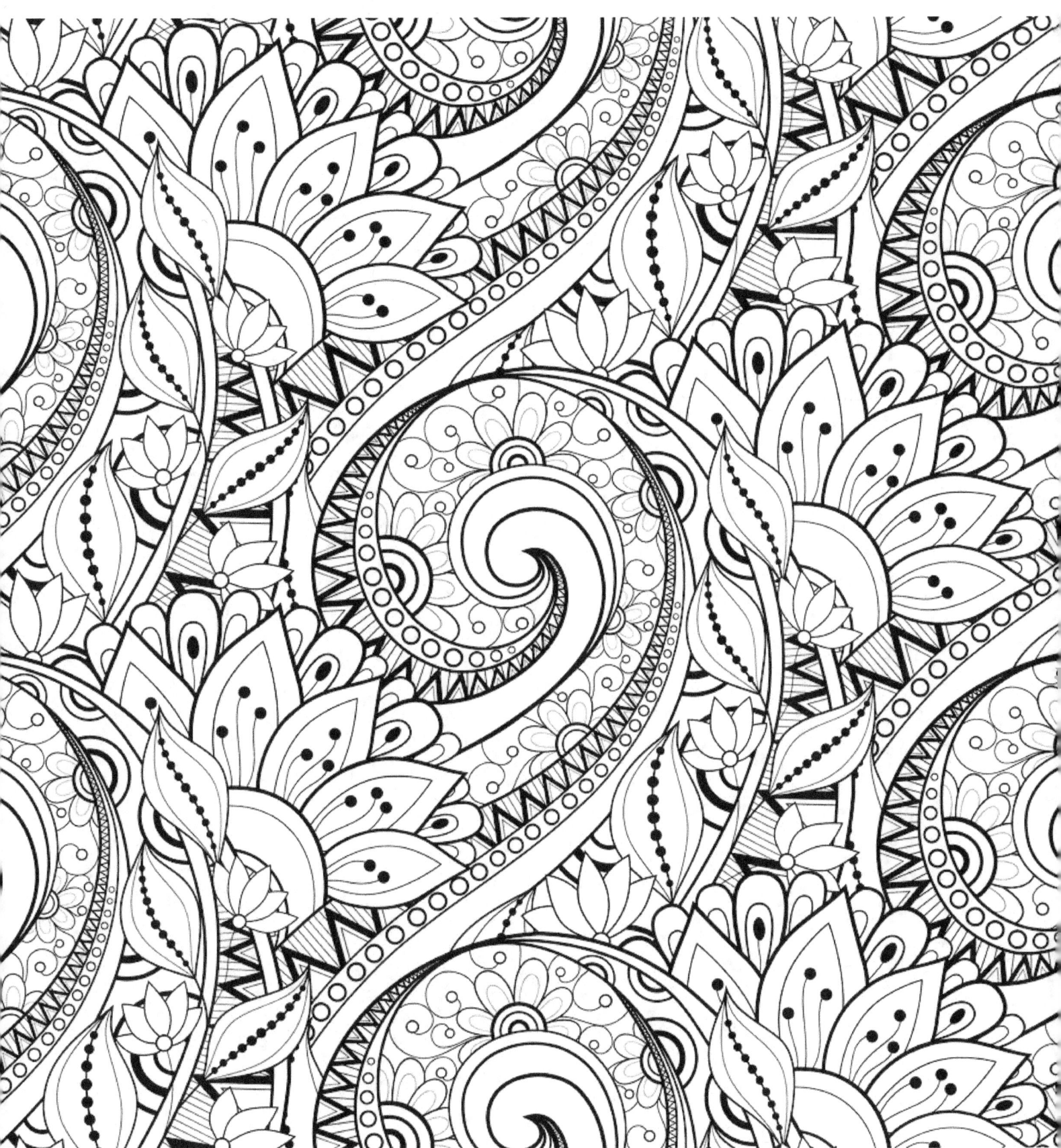

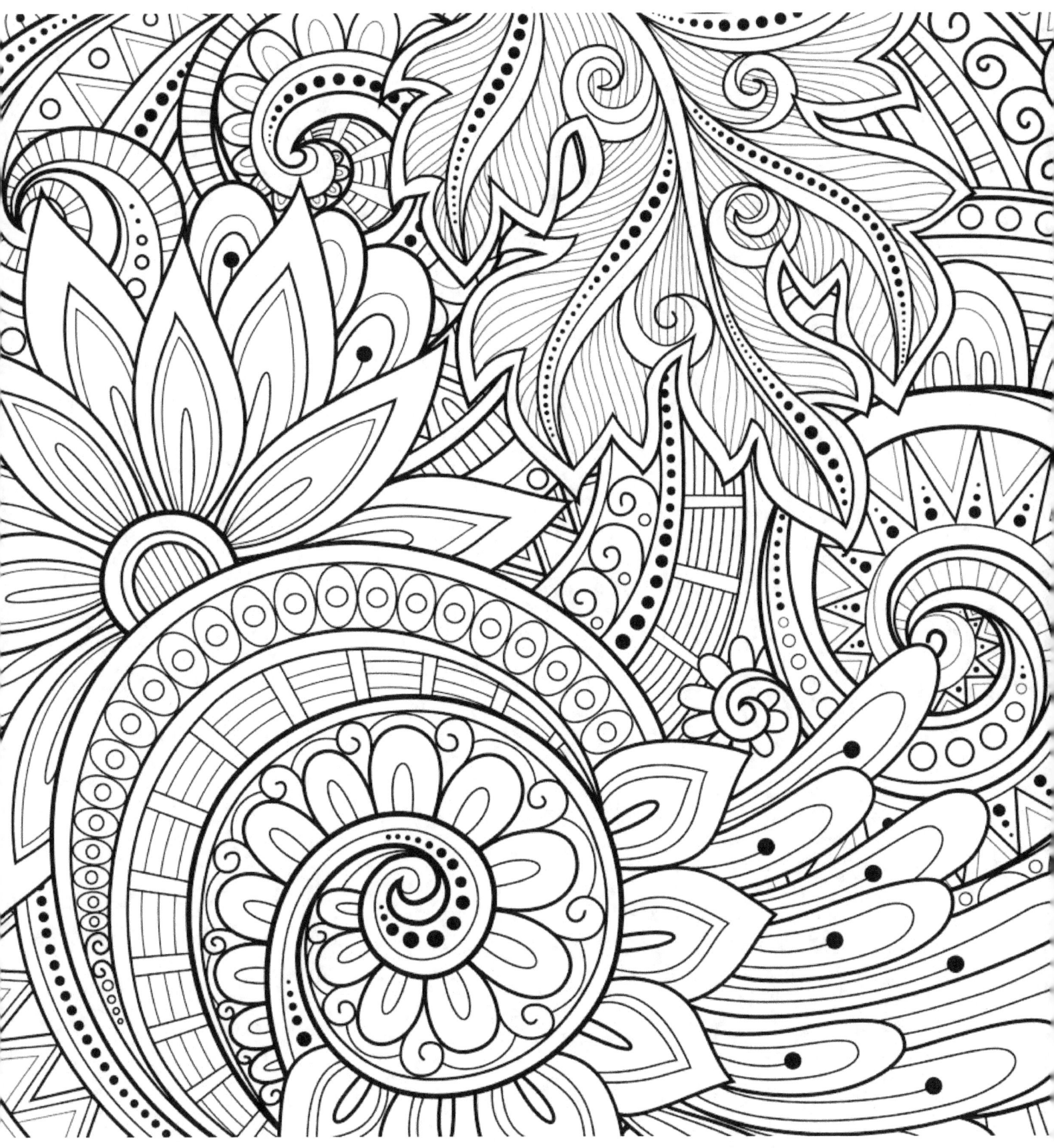

www.ingramcontent.com/pod-product-compliance
Lightning Source LLC
Chambersburg PA
CBHW080742240526
45472CB00025B/2208